If you are looking for a way to
mission in your everyday life, th.
contained in this book will inspire you to seize every—seemingly
ordinary—moment for maximum gospel impact.

—Britney Christian Miller
Christian recording artist and faith blogger

In faith, are we actively participating or sitting on the sidelines? This book
inspires us to recognize, understand, and act on the opportunities that
God presents in our everyday lives. Dr. Montague gives us a game plan
and the confidence to move forward in faith, reminding us that we are on
God's team and He is working through us to be a blessing to others.

—Tommy and Andrea Hottovy
Pitching Coach, Chicago Cubs

Untapped Potential presents a challenge to each reader to examine their
openness and willingness to receive all that God has for them. In a world
of uncertainty and fear, Dr. Montague offers a life in Christ that is not only
rewarding and fruitful, but also essential for today's circumstances. He
displays a balance of practical and supernatural guidelines to accomplish
the work that God has given us to do, along with firsthand experience. He
suggests to tap-in to the spiritual realm and to live a full life in Christ.
A thought-provoking and informative book.

—Connie Engel
Author of *Miracles: Expect Something Wild*

Untapped Potential will alter the way you view every day of your life. God
is bringing people across your path for certain reasons at specific times,
and you have the opportunity to play a part in God's world-changing plan.
Montague's work combines powerful narratives with practical wisdom to
help you identify, act on, and never miss the supernatural possibilities right
in front of you.

—Dr. Jim Miller
Lead Pastor, Real Life Church
Professor, Horizon University

Ryan Montague has produced another powerful book; this text serves
as a wonderful reminder to open our hearts and hands to the leading of
the Holy Spirit. May your life be transformed as you lean into the timeless
principles of this book.

—Dr. Terry Franson
Senior Vice President Emeritus, Azusa Pacific University

Wow! A book that moves you to trust God for the MIRACULOUS in the seemingly mundane conversations of everyday life. It's a book that EVERYONE should read who is looking for practical ways to be used by God. You'll start to see Divine Opportunities EVERYWHERE!

—Anthony and Bonnie Powell
Pastors, Redeemed Life Church

Okay, I'm convicted. This book is a refreshing reminder that my life in Christ is supposed to be a faith adventure. I can plainly see where I have missed opportunities to see God's greatness by failing to be the "Ananias" to a blind Saul of Tarsus in my own sphere of influence. Daring to live out the message in this book bridges the gap between a boring, mundane Christianity and the life of impact God has called us to live.

—Charles Humphrey
Senior Pastor, H.O.P.E.'s House

For those of us who are in the people business (which is everyone!), we have an opportunity to unleash positive change in the lives of many. This book inspires us and tells us how to take advantage of these opportunities. Don't settle for boring, second-hand testimonies. Go after your very own exciting testimony for the glory of God!

—Carlos D. Mayen
Owner/Operator of Chick-fil-A in Azusa, CA

Our dear friend Ryan is truly an agent of change. Read this book and when you are done, read it again to make sure you don't miss any of the nuggets of truth Ryan gives. We were encouraged and challenged to activate even more of God's power in our lives and to never settle for anything other than His very best. You will be too.

—Alex and Shunna Jones-Moreno
Founders of Reach Up Reach Out Ministries

Moving from a Mediocre to a
MIRACULOUS
TESTIMONY

RYAN R. MONTAGUE, PhD

FOREWORD BY DAVID G. WATSON, DMIN

credo
house publishers

Published in the United States by Credo House Publishers,
a division of Credo Communications, LLC, Grand Rapids, Michigan
credohousepublishers.com

All Scripture quotations, unless otherwise indicated, are taken from
the Holy Bible, New International Version®, NIV®. Copyright © 1973,
1978, 1984, 2011 by Biblica, Inc.TM Used by permission of Zondervan.
All rights reserved worldwide. www.zondervan.com. The "NIV" and
"New International Version" are trademarks registered in the United
States Patent and Trademark Office by Biblica, Inc.TM

ISBN: 978-1-62586-162-7

Cover design by Ryan Montague
Interior design by Frank Gutbrod
Editing by Donna Huisjen

Printed in the United States of America

First edition

Dedication

This book is dedicated to my personal Lord and Savior, Jesus Christ. It blows my mind that You would find me worthy of writing these books about You and for You. You constantly surprise me with how personal you are and how much of an intimate relationship you desire with each and every one of us. I pray that your favor is upon this book from cover to cover.

To my wife, Debra, thank you for your love, patience, encouragement, and support. I am blessed beyond measure to have you as a wife, ministry partner, and best friend. Everything God does in and through this book is a part of our shared testimony. I love you and I am so grateful that I get to run this race with you.

To my children David, Makenna, and Bella, being your father has taught me so much about the love of our heavenly Father. I pray that you grow to have your own firsthand experiences with God and a powerful testimony of His activity in your lives. I pray that my life points you to Jesus. Thank you for all your sweet hugs and kisses.

To the Montague and Watson families, thank you for all the love, support, and guidance throughout the years. We are so blessed to have two wonderful families backing us, supporting us, and praying for us.

To Redeemed Life Church and to Pastors Anthony and Bonnie Powell, God has used you as a game-changing divine appointment in my life. You helped bring the Spirit of God into my faith and daily walk. I am forever changed because of your spiritual guidance.

Finally, this book is dedicated to all the Christians out there that are seeking to go to the next-level in their faith. I pray that God uses this book to help you tap into the power of the Holy Spirit and move in the miraculous.

Contents

Foreword

The goal of *Untapped Potential* is to awaken your soul to the divine connections in everyday life. This book is for anyone who desires to experience more God-activity in their life; for anyone who wants to operate in spiritual giftings, not just natural giftings.

Untapped Potential is a beautiful reminder that (1) God doesn't just want to you to do ministry for Him, He wants you to do ministry with Him, (2) God doesn't just want you to experience Him on Sunday, He wants you to experience Him every day, and (3) God doesn't do mediocre, God does miraculous. And this is a season that He wants to call you out of the mediocre and into the miraculous. It's time to shake things up, go after God, and tap into the power of His Holy Spirit. That is why I am excited about this book: it reveals the untapped potential waiting for each and every believer who has the desire to experience God and the courage to give Him a chance.

These miraculous moments aren't just for a select few; they are for all of God's people. The only requirements are openness and obedience to the nudging of the Spirit. God has no favorites and He is the same yesterday, today, and forever. We are to live with the expectation of experiencing biblical activity in our time. I have been blessed with a personal testimony that showcases that God's love and power still reigns. God is for you, with you, and He longs to work through you. This book will help take you the distance.

I first met Ryan when he was beginning his doctorate in communication at the University of Missouri. My initial interest in Ryan was that he was dating my daughter. Around that time, Ryan and Debbie came to church to listen to me preach on divine appointments with God. I will never forget Ryan's immediate interest, which has only grown stronger. Today he and Debbie are married and have blessed my wife and me with three amazing grandchildren.

God has paired Ryan and me for a purpose and a mission. We are both life-long students of divine appointments with a passion for leading others into firsthand experiences with God. I have always said that the Christian faith is a grand adventure with God. It's why I always kept an Indiana Jones hat in my office, to remind me never to let my faith get stagnant but always to pursue the adventure with Christ.

In *Untapped Potential*, Ryan does an excellent job of leading people into the spontaneous fun that there is to be had when you yield your life, daily routine, and conversations to God. Ryan inspires and trains up the next generation of believers to move from a mediocre to a miraculous testimony of the transformative power of the Holy Spirit.

Over the last twelve years, I have had the privilege of watching Ryan grow from lukewarm to on fire, from the mediocre to the miraculous, and there is no one better to lead you on a similar journey. In these pages, Ryan will awaken you to the untapped potential of the power of God. He will help you understand that *you* are the answer to others' prayers and that *you* have the opportunity to partner with a living God to bring transformation in others' lives. Ryan will lead you out of doubtful hesitancy and into bold obedience. He will help you to stop second-guessing God's directives and move you toward courage and obedience. He will help you move in the miraculous as you head out to give others an opportunity to experience a living God.

Dr. David Watson
Former Chair of Pastoral Ministries at North Central University

A Prayer for the Reader

I want to start this book off with a prayer! And not just any prayer, but the same prayer that Paul, Silas, and Timothy prayed for the people of great faith in the church of Thessalonica.

> With this in mind, we constantly pray for
> you, that our God may make you worthy of his
> calling, and that by his power he may bring to
> fruition your every desire for goodness and your
> every deed prompted by faith. We pray this so
> that the name of our Lord Jesus may be glo-
> rified in you, and you in him, according to the
> grace of our God and the Lord Jesus Christ.
> (2 Thessalonians 1:11–12)

Personal Testimony = God's Activity in *Your* Life

Lord, I pray over the person holding and reading this book. I ask that you would lead them and guide them on this journey to experiencing their own firsthand divine opportunities, miracles, and answered prayers.

That this process would be one that grows their personal testimony of your power and love working in them and through them. I pray that this reading would inspire, challenge, and move them in the Spirit.

God, I know that you have so much more that you desire to do, provide, and deliver on in our lives—not in materialistic ways, but in terms of miracles, wonders, and signs. May you soften our hearts and humble our souls so that we can understand you more fully and continue to enjoy your favor. That we may live lives worthy of your call, worthy of your presence in our lives. For your presence among us sets us apart from all other people on the earth. May you fill us with your love and light so that we can shine brightly in the darkness for all to see. We ask that you would go before us and your presence be upon us, so that we can live lives that are attractive, fun, and engaging to the point that people feel compelled to ask and know where our hope and joy come from.

Lord, I ask that you would provide us with clear and effective communication between writer and reader. I ask that you would facilitate the reading process so that this book would be read and received from the place of love that it was written and intended. I ask that you would protect this writing from miscommunication, misunderstanding, and misperception. That in Jesus, this book would be received as it was originally written—with a hope-filled purpose of growing the body of Christ, encouraging and facilitating divine connection in everyday life, and ministering love to all your sons and daughters across the globe.

It's in Jesus' name I pray, AMEN!

Untapped
Potential

Life is like a 10-speed bicycle, most of us
have gears we never use.
—Charles Schulz

A while back, I was thinking about my iPhone and just how little I actually use it. I use about five apps on my iPhone for emails, texts, pictures, calendar reminders, and a little bit of social media scanning. I couldn't help but think of Steve Jobs rolling over in his grave over the fact that he had dedicated his life to creating a pocket-sized power computer with countless features, apps, and abilities, only to have me simply use it for emails, texts, pictures, and calendar reminders. Think about all the untapped applications and features that go unused on a daily basis. The people at Apple would be so disappointed in me. I can hear them yelling, "Why do you even have a smartphone!?! For what you do, just get a flip-phone!"

Have you ever seen someone pull up an app and do something on their smartphone and think to yourself, "No way, I had no idea you could do that? I had no idea it had that app, feature, or ability. That's incredible. How am I just now discovering this!?!"

That's when God convicted me: "Ryan, that's how you approach your faith! I have unimaginable untapped potential for you, and you don't even bother to investigate, explore, or check any of it out." For the first 25 years of my life, I "used" God for two things—as a good luck charm and a listening ear. To which I can hear God saying, "Ryan, for what you use Me for, you don't need a God this big. You of little faith. To those with much faith, I am the God who gives sight to the blind, hearing to the deaf, strength to the paralyzed, and who raises the dead from the grave—I am so much more than you could ever think, hope, or imagine. Ryan, you think you're waiting on Me, but it is the I Am who waits for you (Exodus 3:13-15). I AM here holding what no eye has seen and no ear has heard, waiting on you to broaden your understanding of the power of My Son Jesus. Deepen your faith in the movement of the Holy Spirit and develop a great passion that leads to obedience to My Word."

It wasn't until I was in my mid-thirties that I read four books that forever changed my approach to God—*All In* by Mark Batterson, *Experiencing God* by Henry and Richard Blackaby, *The God I Never Knew* by Robert Morris, and *Translating God* by Shawn Bolz. If you haven't read those books, you MUST! It's weird to promote other books at the start of your own, but you've got to read them. Those books truly helped me understand the involvement, engagement, and excitement that the Holy Spirit wants to bring into our lives, that which is explained and showcased in the book of Acts. That's when I had the thought: "No way!!! I had no idea you could do that through the Holy Spirit!?! I had no idea the Holy Spirit offered those applications, features, and abilities. That's incredible! How am I just now discovering the power of the Holy Spirit!" I was exceedingly frustrated after I had discovered all this. I felt genuinely robbed that no one had ever sat me down and explained to me the power of the Holy Spirit and the untapped potential in my God.

Here's an excerpt from *Experiencing God* that does a wonderful job of explaining what God can do in and through *ordinary people*:

> When you think about working with God in His mission to redeem the lost world, you may ask, "What can one ordinary person do?" One of the wonderful Scriptures that helped me on this point describes Elijah: "Elijah was a man with a nature like ours; yet he prayed earnestly that it would not rain, and for three years and six months it did not rain on the land. Then he prayed again, and the sky gave rain and the land produced its fruit" (James 5:17–18).

This mighty man of God was an ordinary person just like you and me. But when he prayed, God responded miraculously. Elijah did not have any unusual giftedness or power. He simply humbled himself in the role of servant. He obeyed everything God instructed him to do, and God worked through Elijah to influence an entire nation to return to God.

Peter and John were two of the first disciples Jesus called to follow Him. After Jesus' resurrection, God healed a crippled beggar through Peter. Peter and John were called before the Sanhedrin—the highest court in the land—to give an account of their actions. Filled with the Holy Spirit, Peter spoke fearlessly to the religious leaders. Notice the people's response: "When they observed the boldness of Peter and John and realized that they were uneducated and untrained men, they were amazed and knew that they had been with Jesus" (Acts 4:13).

Most of the people we read about in the Scriptures were ordinary men and women. Their relationships with God and God's activity in their lives made them extraordinary. Did you notice the statement—the leaders recognized that Peter and John "had been with Jesus"? Peter and John were common fishermen, but their association with Jesus made them world changers. Anyone who enters into an intimate relationship with God can see God do exceptional things through his or her life. The outcome does not depend upon a person being unusually gifted, educated, or wealthy. The key is the indwelling presence of God doing unusual things through a willing servant.

The main theme from my first book, *Divine Opportunity*, focused around a quote from the philosopher Martin Buber: "There are no gifted or ungifted here, only those who give themselves versus those who withhold themselves." And this holds true as the center point for this book as well. The extraordinary divine opportunity stories you will read in this book are from ordinary men and women whose obedience put them in a position to be used by the Holy Spirit. The sometimes hard-to-read missed opportunity stories in this book are from ordinary men and women whose disobedience kept them from being used by the Holy Spirit. It's that simple.

Tapping into the Holy Spirit

Here's the thing I've realized: teaming up with the Holy Spirit is like playing a two-on-two basketball game with LeBron James as your teammate. You can do next to nothing and still win! All you have to do is enter the game, step onto the court, and let Bron Bron take it from there. Your height, age, race, intelligence, job title, and ability do not matter one bit. No matter who you are, if we pair you with LeBron and go pick any two people from the nearest office building, coffee shop, or shopping center to be your opponents, you and LeBron will dominate. It's a guaranteed win. The same goes for teaming up with the Holy Spirit. All you have to do is enter the game of life and step into conversation with people, then let the Holy Spirit take it from there. But we do indeed have to step out and give God a chance! Ultimately, when we partner with the Holy Spirit, all of a sudden we are forces to be reckoned with. Forces of encouragement, support, wisdom, love, and grace. *When we partner with the Holy Spirit, we go from ordinary men and women to agents of God's mighty power.*

> For the Kingdom of God is not just a lot of talk;
> it is living by God's power. (1 Corinthians 4:20 NLT)

The problem is that, more often than not, we withhold ourselves rather than give ourselves to divine opportunities, and *we live in bondage to our weakness rather than in the light of God's power.* And far too many Christians can think of more stories from their own experience of missed opportunities than of divine appointments. Let me give you a couple of examples of missed opportunities so that you can have some perspective on the wide range of moments that can fall into this category.

One missed opportunity that stands out in my life was from ten years ago. At the time I was in my third year of my doctoral program at the University of Missouri. Ironically enough, I was in the beginning stages of my dissertation research on divine appointments and missed opportunities.

On this particular weekend, I had driven from Columbia, Missouri, where I was living, to Kansas City, Missouri, where I had grown up. Some good, lifelong friends of mine were hosting a soccer tournament, Kickin' for Kids, to raise funds and awareness for the Children's Mercy Hospital. I had participated and helped out in the event on Saturday afternoon and was driving back home to Columbia, Missouri, on Sunday morning to pick my wife up and get to church.

I left Kansas City at about 8:00 a.m. Sunday morning. Keep in mind that this is the middle of July in Missouri, so even at 8:00 a.m. it's already 80 degrees and 80% humidity. As I am driving east on the stretch of highway out of town, I look across the other side of the highway, headed west, and see a pregnant woman walking along the side of the highway in flip-flops. Now, I'm smart enough not to go around randomly guessing whether women are pregnant. Which means that this woman was super pregnant; we're not talking about a little bump that could just have been a big breakfast. We're talking end-of-term pregnancy.

I think to myself, "What on earth is she doing walking on the side of the highway, fully pregnant, by herself, in the middle of summer? Then I think, "Surely, someone else driving on her side of the highway will stop and pick her up." Then the thought comes to me: "What if everyone else is thinking the same thing as me—'Surely, someone else will . . .' —and then no one does?"

So, I take the next exit, pull around the highway, and head back in the opposite direction. I pull over a little ways in front of her and wait for her to walk up toward my truck. I roll the window down and ask if I can give her a ride. She gladly accepts and gets into my truck. I ask whether everything is okay and where she wants me to take her. She says she had gone into the hospital last night because she was concerned about her pregnancy. But after some tests and checkups, she was released this morning to go home. She couldn't get ahold of anyone to come and pick her up, so she just started walking. She planned on walking a little ways and then calling some more people.

Come to find out, not only is she pregnant but her due date is the next week. I can't believe she doesn't have someone with her, let alone someone who will at least pick her up. I think about my wife and sister and how they would have multiple people willing to go with them to hospital, stay at the hospital, and definitely give them a ride home. I see one red flag after another that this woman's home situation is not the best.

I ask her, "Where can I take you?" She says, "Oh, just a little ways down the highway and you can drop me off." I reply, "I'm happy to take you all the way home—just tell me where to go." So I do. And we end up driving 15 miles!

As we drive, she talks about how she was originally from Liberty, Missouri, a nice small suburb of Kansas City, and how much she wanted to get back there. This is as we are finally pulling off the highway and driving through one of the sketchier parts of the bigger city. We pass several abandoned buildings with smashed windows and low-income housing.

We finally pull up and park near her duplex. As we are finishing our conversation, I feel this internal prompting to ask if she is okay, offer to pray for her, and even take her someplace else instead. But for whatever reason I just can't get myself to blurt it out. Instead, I just wish her well, say goodbye, and do the wimpy Christian thing of tagging a muddled "God bless" onto the end. She walks off, I drive off, and I've wondered to this day what kind of home environment she walked into and how she is doing.

Here are some ways I have come to define missed opportunities. *Missed opportunities* could be times when you felt prompted by God to start a conversation but didn't. They could be times when you felt prompted by God in the middle of a conversation to ask a hard question or turn the conversation in a more serious direction but didn't. They could be times in conversation when you did something ordinary when God wanted to do something extraordinary. Finally, missed opportunities could be times when you told yourself you had done enough to help, but in the end you knew you didn't.

I Didn't Do Enough to Help

Shortly after this missed opportunity, I was watching the movie *42*, the story of Jackie Robinson, the first African-American professional baseball player to break the color barrier in Major League Baseball by playing for the Brooklyn Dodgers. I was pretty familiar with Jackie Robinson's story. However, I was not familiar with the story of Branch Rickey, the general manager of the Brooklyn Dodgers. The movie highlights a little bit of Branch Rickey's story and how it was his idea and desire to be the manager of the team that broke the color barrier. And it was Mr. Rickey who handpicked Jackie Robinson for the job.

In the middle of the movie is a scene between Robinson and Rickey. Robinson turns to Mr. Rickey and asks, "Why did you do this for me?" Mr. Rickey responds by sharing a missed opportunity from many years earlier that had fueled his passion for the cause. He says,

> I love baseball. I've given my whole life to it. Forty odd years ago, I was a player-coach at Ohio Wesleyan University. We had a [black] catcher, best hitter on the team. I saw him laid low, broken because of the color of his skin. And I didn't do enough to help. I told myself that I did, but I didn't. There was something unfair at the heart of the game I loved, and I ignored it. Then a time came when I could no longer do that.

That line has stuck with me ever since, "I didn't do enough to help. I told myself that I did, but I didn't." And that's exactly how I felt leaving that pregnant woman that day: "I did more than many other people would have done, but I didn't do as much as what Jesus had put in my heart to do." And I felt as though I had let down the woman, myself, and God (who loves the woman).

Here is one more missed opportunity story to give you some perspective on the range and severity of some of these moments. This story comes from Tim, a pastor in the Midwest.

When I was in college, I worked for Young Life, which is an evangelistic, relationship-based ministry for high school students. One of Young Life's mottos is "You have to earn the right to be heard." I think that at times when I was in college, I misconstrued that to mean "I need to get into their life as a friend first, before I start sharing anything with them."

I worked in a high school that was right on the edge of the inner city and suburbs. So it was like a melting pot of wealthier suburban students, lower-income city students, and everyone in between. One of the students I worked with was one of the suburban kids, but he had this unique ability to relate to every single one of those groups at the high school. Everybody loved him. Honestly, when I first met him it was hard to become friends with him because he was being pulled in several different directions. But I thought, "Man, this kid is going to be a key person for me to get onboard. If I become friends with him, I'm going to be able to get all his friends to come to Young Life."

But I was misconstruing "You need to earn the right to be heard." So I didn't really take the time to dig into his spiritual life before the rest of it. And several times I really felt like God convicted me of that, just saying, "You need to have that conversation. You need to start digging into his life spiritually instead of just befriending him all the time." But I was always really nervous. I didn't want to push him away. I didn't want to have that conversation and him go, "Dude, I'm not having that conversation with you" and then just be done with it. So I never did.

There was one moment in particular that stands out. It was at his lacrosse practice. He played lacrosse for the high school, and the area director for Young Life was his lacrosse coach. So I ended up at practice one day, and it just so happened that this young man had been suspended for the week because of something academic—tardies or misconduct type of thing. This particular day we were both sitting on the sidelines, watching practice together and shooting the breeze.

Then he brought up not really understanding how God works and why He allows certain things to happen. I can remember just sitting there thinking, "This is the door that's opening for me to talk to him." I really did feel like this was my chance. We did talk about God for a little while, but I never just stopped and said, "Hey, you know, God loves you and wants a relationship with you." I don't know why I didn't. I think in the back of my mind I was just saying, "I don't want to push him too hard. I don't want to push him too hard."

Then before I knew it we were on to talking about somebody's car and then quickly on to something else. That was definitely the one clear moment I remember. It was just me and him. No one else was around. We were just sitting there talking. And I missed it.

As a result of skipping these harder, more challenging conversations, I missed the fact that he was actually very depressed. And about three weeks later he had a fight with his parents. He was out at a party and his parents wanted him to come home, but he wanted to stay out later. His parents ended up driving over to the party and pretty much dragging him out, embarrassing him in front of his friends.

After that he was really upset and shaken. On top of that he was dealing with his depression, which he kept closed off about. Then one day, while his parents were out, he took his dad's belt and hung himself in a tree in the backyard.

After I found out about all that, an extreme amount of guilt came onto me, and I was really hard on myself afterward for quite some time. Just thinking about my opportunity and how I had let it pass right by. I couldn't help but just play that conversation over and over again in my mind. Luckily, I had some good friends who didn't allow me to take on all that shame and kept me grounded and rooted in God. But after that experience, I have become more bold, honest, and direct. I'd rather risk hurting someone's feelings by pressing a little too hard than miss another opportunity like that as a result of not pressing hard enough.

Unfortunately, Tim is not the only person who has shared that kind of a heartbreaking missed opportunity. In thirty interviews, six people shared times when they felt as though they'd had a clear opening to dive into deeper spiritual conversation and missed it. Shortly after those missed moments, three of the individuals with whom they had declined to enter into conversation had committed suicide, one had died in a car accident, one had died in a house fire, and one had died from a terminal illness. This is hard to write, hard to read, and harder yet to live. It's these challenging missed opportunities that people often need help unpacking and understanding. I'll get into more of that in the chapters in Part Two of this book.

But for now, we need to realize that these missed opportunities can range from anything as mild as missing an opportunity to give someone a few dollars for gas outside a gas station to missing an opportunity to pray for someone before they head into a potentially fatal surgery. Regardless of the perceived level of severity, we all miss opportunities—likely every single day. Most of them we don't even notice because we are too busy keeping to our schedule and too distracted by our smartphone.

Occasionally, when I ask people about their own missed opportunities, I hear them say, "You know what—I don't think I've had any missed opportunities." And I'm like, "Who are you, Jesus junior?" We've all missed opportunities! And we've all likely missed opportunities today! When people deny this, it usually signifies to me that their heart and mind are so far out of the game that they don't even realize they're missing opportunities.

A Heart-Check and Wakeup Call

We all need a heart-check and wakeup call to the divine opportunities God presents us with each day. Unfortunately, it's often the people who have experienced the most tragic missed opportunities who are the most alert and obedient moving forward. Those who've had the hardest missed opportunities tend to go on to have the most amazing divine appointments. As Tim said above, "I'd rather risk hurting someone's feelings by pressing a little too hard than miss another opportunity like that as a result of not pressing hard enough."

If you are one of those people who doesn't think you've missed any opportunities, then this book is absolutely for you. However, I will warn you that being awakened to the missed opportunities swirling around you won't always be pleasant. It's often a hard awakening to the reality of our selfishness, disregard for people, and disobedience to God.

If you are one of those people who has taken a pass on a big missed opportunity, as Tim did, then this book is absolutely for you. And I will walk you through the healing process that is needed to overcome that missed opportunity by experiencing the good grief and good discipline from God, then asking for and receiving God's grace and forgiveness, and finally moving forth with a healthy level of motivation from your past experiences.

I can't wait for you to have your eyes and ears opened to the opportunities all around you. And to live a life in which you minimize the number of missed opportunities and maximize the number of divine appointments. *Let us no longer lead lives of untapped potential and instead tap into the power of the Holy Spirit to see and engage people with the heart of Christ.*

Below is a story from my neighbor Mike, a sixty-year-old Mexican-American who works for the city doing maintenance. Mike was one of those readers of my first book, *Divine Opportunity*, who had his eyes and ears opened to the divine moments all around him. Prior to reading the book, Mike already had the heart of Christ and had experienced the power of the Holy Spirit after God had miraculously rescued him from a severe drug addiction many years earlier. However, it was more recently that he had begun to apply his heart of Christ and the power of the Holy Spirit to the divine opportunities of everyday life. Recalls Mike,

It was Good Friday. My wife, Sharon, and I were heading out to run some errands. Before we had driven away, my neighbor Charles flagged us down. I have known Charles for many years. Our boys, who are now in their thirties, grew up playing sports against each other, and we've had an ongoing friendship ever since. Charles lives across the street with his wife, Lori, and her dad. Her dad at this time was in his lower nineties and was bedridden.

So, when Charles flagged us down, we pulled over at the end of his driveway. He said to me, "Hey Mike, I have a favor to ask. I know you're a very religious man." My wife and I later laughed about that, because that would not at all have been how I would have seen myself. But I said, "Okay, what can I do for you?" Charles replied, "My father-in-law is not doing very well. With that new law that California passed that people can do assisted suicide, he's going to go ahead and take himself out."

Sharon and I were a little frightened by the idea of somebody taking their own life based on their choosing. Charles continued, "I just wanted to see if you could come by and maybe pray with my father-in-law." I said, "When would you like me to do that?" He answered, "Maybe sometime after Sunday." I replied, "Well, I could come in right now." Charles replied, "No, that's okay." So we left that moment with very loose plans and nothing specific nailed down.

As we drove off, I shared with my wife that I thought I needed to be more proactive than that and see what God would want me to do. So we ran our errands and came back home. I told my wife I needed to go and pray and seek God about this. I prayed that God would give me the courage to call Charles and ask if I could do this sooner rather than later. But most importantly, I prayed that the Holy Spirit would give me the courage to do this, because this is not something I do all the time.

I gave Charles a call, but he said, "Not right now—we've got family over right now. Maybe sometime toward the beginning of the week." I said, "Well, there's no guarantee that the timing will work out the way we want it to." He said, "It's okay, we'll find time at the beginning of the week." I told Sharon and we prayed that God would open up an opportunity because we were still worried about this assisted suicide.

The next day, Saturday of Easter weekend, Charles called me: "Hey, you know, I've been thinking about it more. Do you think you could come over now? We still have family here, but it would be okay." I said, "Absolutely." I grabbed my Bible, looked up a few verses to share, and prayed again that God would give me the words to say and keep me from saying anything that would not be from Him. I asked God, "I need You to do for me what You did for Moses. Because I really hate public speaking and reading in front of others. And I'm not good about sharing about Jesus in front of a group of family members like this." I knew that Moses had a stutter and that God had still used him and worked through him. I asked God to do that for me.

When I got over there and walked into the father's room, there was a handful of family members in there. My first thought was, "Oh no! What have I gotten myself into? This is way beyond my comfort zone." But I remembered that Charles had said I was a religious man, so I didn't want to let him or God down. I had prayed that God would give me courage, so I knew I needed to step up and do this.

I turned to the father, lying there in his bed, introduced myself, and began to share with him about Christ. Again, I absolutely dread reading in front of people, so this was a major stretch for me. I read and shared with him John 3:16, that God so loved the world that He sent His one and only Son, so that whoever believes in Him will not perish but have eternal life. I also read and shared all of Psalm 23 that the Lord is my shepherd; I have all that I need . . . and will live in the house of the Lord forever.

You've got to understand, this was a long reading for me in a group like that. As I've said, I'm not a public reader. I don't even like to read a menu. This was well beyond my comfort zone, but I was acting in God's courage.

As I read and shared with him, I stopped to confirm with him twice that he understood what I was saying and who Jesus

Christ is. Then I told him, "If you accept Jesus Christ as your Lord and Savior, your name will be written in the Book of Life. You'll go on to live in eternity with the Lord." He nodded yes the first time I asked. But I needed to hear him say yes. So when I asked him the second time, "Do you accept Jesus Christ as your Lord and Savior?" he actually said yes out loud. When he finally did, that took the pressure off, and I thought, "Okay, Lord. Your job is done here."

I thanked the father for letting me share with him about Jesus. That's how I felt, thankful that I'd had the opportunity to share about Christ. Then I prayed for him and the rest of the family who were in the room. Afterward, when I left to go back home across the street, I felt like I was floating! It was such an incredible feeling.

The next morning, which happened to be Easter Sunday, I received a call from Charles. He called to tell me that his father-in-law had passed away in his sleep that night. No drugs. No assisted suicide. He had died naturally. I couldn't believe God's timing. About twelve hours after praying with this man and his acceptance of Jesus Christ, he had passed away in his sleep. Praise God!

I love this testimony of God's never-ending pursuit of His children all the way to the final days, hours, and minutes of their lives. It's amazing what God will do with us and through us when we are open and obedient to the opportunities He puts in front of us. All it took was one faithful follower to *tap into the courage of Christ* to go and give an opportunity for a dying neighbor to experience God and go on to live with Him in eternity. Praise God!

New Lessons Since Divine Opportunity

This book, in many ways, is an extension of *Divine Opportunity*. This book contains new lessons learned and stories lived about Divine Opportunities and Missed Opportunities since the publication of the first book. Is it helpful to have read *Divine Opportunity* first?—Yes. Is it vital to read *Divine Opportunity* first?—No. I have full confidence that you will be blessed tremendously by the lessons and stories in this book, even without any prior knowledge on this topic. And I wholeheartedly believe that if you put these principles into practice you will see your faith strengthen and grow in ways that cannot be achieved without your own firsthand experiences with God, Jesus, and the Holy Spirit.

The first section of this book, "Untapped Potential," contains chapters that unpack the various reasons we miss opportunities and what impact this has on us and others. The second section of the book, "Moving from Missed Opportunity to Heart Transformation," contains chapters that will outline the process of healing after missing opportunities for potential divine appointments. This requires moving from guilt and conviction to asking for and receiving God's grace and forgiveness to going forth to experience redemptive moments. The third section of this book, "Go and Give Opportunity," contains chapters that will teach you practical steps for engaging in your own firsthand divine opportunities.

DISCUSSION QUESTIONS

1. Charles Schulz said, "Life is like a 10-speed bicycle, most of us have gears we never use." What are some of the gears of God (spiritual gifts, miracles, or divine engagement) that you would like to go after? What are some of the untapped potential or gears of God that you wish you had discovered earlier in life?

2. What is one experience from your past when you truly felt you had partnered with the Holy Spirit to accomplish something beyond your own capabilities? What is one challenge you are anticipating in the present or future for which you will need the power of the Holy Spirit to follow through?

3. What is one experience from your past when you felt as though you had missed an opportunity or left an encounter telling yourself that you had done enough to help—knowing that you had not? What lesson did you learn from this missed opportunity?

Firsthand Experiences with God

Give someone a fish and you feed them for a day.
Teach someone to fish and you feed them for a lifetime.
—Adage

Since the publication of my first book, *Divine Opportunity*, the greatest lesson I have learned is the power of firsthand experiences with God. In *Divine Opportunity*, chapter 8, "Optimistic Obedience," I shared this statement from a young woman following her own divine appointment:

> There are a lot of people out there just like me, who need to experience God firsthand. There are too many people living on the secondhand experiences of other people. I needed this firsthand experience with God. I needed to be reminded that God Himself really does care about me personally.

I have since come to realize just how profound and important her statement is to the life, faith, and the ministry of every Christian. Have you heard the maxim, "Give someone a fish and you feed them for a day. Teach someone to fish and you feed them for a lifetime"? God has been reinforcing in me that if you share a divine opportunity story with someone you will feed them spiritually for a day. But if you teach someone to experience their own divine opportunities you will feed them spiritually for a lifetime! This has become my life's calling, passion, and desire. This is the journey I would like to take you on throughout this book.

My wife and I have been overwhelmed by the life-changing impact reported to us by readers of *Divine Opportunity* who have pressed in and experienced what ONLY God could do. I have no doubt you will have a similar experience during and after reading this book. *God does not play favorites. God doesn't equip and allow only certain types of Christians to experience these firsthand divine appointments.* It's God's heart and desire that every believer experience their own divine opportunities. It's not about being gifted or ungifted; it's about those who faithfully give themselves versus those who reluctantly withhold themselves.

> There will be . . . glory, honor and peace for
> everyone who does good: first for the Jew,
> then for the Gentile. For God does not show
> favoritism. (Romans 2:9–11)

It's a great feeling to know that we are all God's favorites and that He will use anyone and everyone who has a willing heart! When you read the Bible, you see that God did not have a high, selective standard of intelligence, wealth, ability, or prestige in order for Him to utilize someone to advance His kingdom. God used shepherds; fishermen; tax collectors; and, most importantly, a carpenter. The only requirement is to have a heart for God.

Power in the Firsthand Experience with God

This journey starts by recognizing the limits of living off the secondhand experiences of others' faith, as opposed to the dynamic power of having your own firsthand experiences with God. In John 4:1–42 we are presented with the story of Jesus and the Samaritan woman meeting and talking at the water well. (If you are not familiar with the story, I encourage you to stop and read it.) As Jesus sits and talks with the

Samaritan woman, she receives a firsthand experience with God. Jesus calls her out on the deepest, darkest secrets of her life: she has had five husbands in the past and isn't married to the man she is living with now. Then Jesus reveals himself as the Messiah she has been waiting on. The Samaritan woman leaves with this deeply personal testimony of connecting with Christ. John writes in 4:28–30, 39–42:

> Leaving her water jar, the woman went back to the town and said to the people,
>
> "Come, see a man who told me everything I ever did. Could this be the Messiah?"
>
> They came out of the town and made their way toward him. . . .
>
> Many of the Samaritans from that town believed in him because of the woman's testimony, "He told me everything I ever did." So when the Samaritans came to him, they urged him to stay with them, and he stayed two days. And because of his words many more became believers.
>
> They said to the woman, "*We no longer believe just because of what you said; now we have heard for ourselves, and we know that this man really is the Savior of the world.*" (emphasis added)

This is the power of firsthand experience with God. Having a secondhand experience with God through hearing a testimony of another believer is wonderful, encouraging, and inspiring—for a short while. Hearing secondhand experiences of God creates interest, curiosity, and wonder. *Having your own firsthand experience with God is a spiritual game changer!* You walk away saying, "Now I know that Jesus is indeed the Savior of the world." Firsthand experiences with God create confidence, connection, and unwavering faith. I'm begging you to wholeheartedly pursue these firsthand experiences with God. Your life and faith will never be the same.

There is spiritual danger in settling for secondhand experiences with God. Let me give you an example. I once heard a pastor, at a baby dedication, pray for the child to have a boring testimony. Now, I know what the pastor meant. I know that he was praying for a life without deep troubles—drugs, addiction, poor choices with lasting consequences, and distant wandering from God. But that prayer caused me to take a step back for a moment and reflect upon my prayers for my own children. I realized that a boring testimony is going to get you only so far in your relationship with God. As Mark Batterson says, "Holiness is not just doing nothing wrong, it's doing something right. You can do nothing wrong, and still do nothing right." And ultimately, *a boring testimony leads to a boring faith.*

Personal Testimony = God's Activity in *Your* Life

Pray for an Exciting and Thrilling Testimony

We must all strive for an exciting and thrilling testimony. One that is filled with firsthand experiences of Scripture that comes alive, radical love for our neighbor, answered prayers, miracles, and divine appointments. I want a crazy awesome testimony of God's favor, provision, freedom, and saving grace. As Mark Batterson puts it, I want to be able to share story after story of how "God has showed up and showed off" in my life. Parents, you MUST have an exciting testimony to share with your children, whether it's overcoming deep brokenness or experiencing great provision or both. By provision I mean radical love, answered prayers, divine appointments, and miracles. Your children need to get excited about what God the Father, Jesus, and the Holy Spirit have done in your lives. And children/young adults of the family, you need to experience your own firsthand testimonies about what God the Father, Jesus, and the Holy Spirit have done in your lives. *When there's no wonder in activity with God, we wander from God.*

Boring testimonies from parents will lead to boring faith for their children. Boring faith for children will lead to a wandering from God. On the other hand, exciting testimonies from parents will lead to genuine curiosity about faith in their children. Genuine curiosity about faith in their children will lead to exciting firsthand adventures with God. And *exciting firsthand adventures with God are vital to the life of faith for every Christian.*

A while back I watched the movie *Hacksaw Ridge*. It is a war story from World War II based on the true story of Desmond Doss (warning: portions of the movie are rather gruesome and not for the faint of heart). Doss, a Christian—a Seventh Day Adventist—refused to touch a weapon, let alone carry one. He entered the military as a conscientious objector and sought to become a medic to help save lives instead of taking lives. His refusal to carry a weapon caused a lot of backlash from his commanders and comrades, who deemed him a coward. Despite much hazing, Doss pushed through and served as a medic. It was in the battle of Okinawa, Japan, that over the course of one night Doss risked his own life to rescue and save 75 of his wounded comrades, while he himself was under fire and under attack. He would later receive the Medal of Honor for this remarkable act of heroism.

When I looked up the movie online, I read an interview with Producer Mel Gibson. Gibson said that he'd had to leave portions of Doss's real life out of the movie, because had he included it all, audiences would have thought it too hard to believe. That's the kind of testimony I want to have with God. If someone were to tell the story of my life at the end of my days, I would want them to have to leave out stories of divine opportunities because audiences would find them too miraculous or simply too frequent to believe. And I want the same thing for you! Because a thrilling testimony leads to a dynamic faith. A boring testimony leads to a stale faith.

Here's an illustration of the power of firsthand experience with God. This story comes from my father-in-law, Pastor David Watson:

I have established a routine of preaching at the same 5–7 churches throughout the Midwest each summer. Two years ago I was at a church in Arkansas. I preached on the topic of divine appointments and shared a couple of my own divine opportunity stories and encouraged people to go out and experience their own.

After the service a man approached to speak and pray with me. As he began to speak, it was obvious that he had a severe stutter. And it was through his stutter that he expressed sadness, disappointment, and frustration that he felt as though he could never experience a divine appointment. He thought that because of his stutter no one would take him seriously or have the patience for him in a divine moment like that. He desperately desired a divine appointment conversation but was grieved and felt plagued by his stutter. I encouraged him and offered to pray with him that God would gift him with a divine appointment conversation as he so much desired.

Since I visit this church only once each summer, it was a whole year before I returned to preach. After I had preached the following summer, the man with the stutter approached me again. And this is the story he shared:

"Last year you prayed for me to have a divine appointment of my own. So I was on the lookout for any possible divine opportunities. A couple of weeks later I found myself in a checkout line at the local Dollar General store. I was waiting in line behind this large, intimidating man. Just then a woman stepped in line behind me. She recognized me from church, and we began to talk about our church. Just then the big, intimidating man turned, looked at us, and said, 'You know what, church is for weak people!' And he turned right back around.

"I really felt like this might be a divine opportunity, but I couldn't quite bring myself to say anything. Before I knew it, he had checked out and left. I then checked out and headed off to my car. As I walked out, the big guy was standing by his truck, which was parked right next to my car, smoking a cigarette. I again thought this might be a divine opportunity. As I approached him, I tried to muster all the courage I had to share a thought with him, despite my severe stutter. As I got close, I said, 'You, you, you know what? Ga, Ga, Ga, God loves you. An, an, an, an, and God misses you. An, an, an, and He wants to meet you at chu, chu, chu, church.'

"He just stared at me, took one last drag on his cigarette, flicked it near my feet, hopped into his truck, and without saying a word sped off out of the parking lot. I thought to myself, 'See, God will never be able to use me with this stutter.' I felt defeated and frustrated.

"About a month later I was out to eat with my wife and mother-in-law at a local buffet. We had all gone up to fill our plates. I happened to be the first one to sit back down. As I did I looked up, and walking toward me was the big, intimidating guy with all the tattoos. I just thought to myself, 'Oh, no. Not here. Not in front of my wife and mother-in-law.'

"Just then, as he approached the table, he stuck out his hand. So I hesitantly stuck out mine and we shook hands. He then said, 'I just have to thank you! I know that it must have taken some courage for you to approach me that day in the parking lot of the Dollar General. But I'm glad you did. Later that week, my thirteen-year-old daughter, who means the world to me, was invited to church by some close friends. When she was at church that day, she accepted Christ as her Savior. She came home all excited about the experience, and she said to me, "Dad, God loves you and God misses you. And He wants to meet you at church." The same line you had shared that day in the parking lot. The next Sunday I went to church with her, and I ended up accepting Christ. So I just wanted to thank you for having the courage to speak to me that day. I know that with your stutter and my attitude, that must have been tough.' Then he left.

"Later my wife, who had watched this conversation from a distance, walked up and asked about the interaction. I told her the whole story about my desire for a divine appointment of my own, meeting this guy at the Dollar General, and all that he had shared that day. My wife just looked at me, stunned, much more than the story warranted. I asked, 'What's a matter?' She said, 'Honey, you're not stuttering anymore!!!'

"From that moment on, I've never stuttered since."

Can you believe that!?! Talk about a firsthand, life-altering encounter with the living God. There's no doubt this man's faith is forever changed after an experience like that. And his family will receive that spiritual legacy as well. Scripture tells us that our nourishment comes from doing the will of God and from finishing His work (John 4:34). "For we are God's handiwork, created in Christ Jesus to do good works, which God prepared in advance for us to do" (Ephesians 2:10). "Therefore [we] glory in Christ Jesus in [our] service to God. [We] will not venture to speak of anything except what Christ has accomplished through [us]" (Romans 15:17–18). Can I get an AMEN!?!

Christianity Is So Much Fun

God doesn't just want you to observe the faith, He wants you to participate in the faith. When you live your faith and participate in a divine opportunity, it's contagious and leaves you hungry for more. When you simply observe the faith, it can become boring and stale. For example, I grew up playing soccer, my club team won a state championship my senior year of high school, and I went on to play a little in college. I LOVE playing soccer! Even now in my late thirties, I love playing soccer. But I'll be honest: watching soccer is incredibly boring for me—sorry, soccer fans. Sure, there might be a few exciting moments in the course of ninety minutes, but not enough to keep me sustained and interested.

I feel as though there is great overlap in the life of faith. When you are engaged and participating, faith comes alive—it's exciting and contagious. But if you are merely watching and observing the life of faith, it will not be enough. There might be a few exciting moments, but not enough to keep you sustained and engaged. Think about it: Who's most engaged and excited on game day, the starters or the benchwarmers? The starters, of course, because they know they're a part of the action and the outcome. God wants you to be a starter. God wants you to participate in the action and relish the outcome! God wants you on fire for doing good works!

Our nourishment comes from doing the will of God and finishing His work (John 4:34). "For we are God's handiwork, created in Christ

Jesus to do good works, which God prepared in advance for us to do" (Ephesians 2:10). We have reason to be enthusiastic about all Christ Jesus has done through us in our service to God. Notice the participative language in these verses. We are created and called to DO the will of God, to DO the good works God prepared for us to DO. The result: we have a reason to be ENTHUSIASTIC about Christ (Romans 15:17–18). *When we DO good works and DO the will of God, we become ENTHUSIASTIC about Christ, and Christianity becomes so much FUN!!!*

Take the apostle Peter, for example; he didn't just observe Jesus' life and ministry. No, Peter got to participate with Him. When the apostles found Jesus walking on top of the water, Peter got to walk out on the water with Jesus! Until he got scared by the wind and waves, wimped out, and started to drown, of course, but either way there are still only two people in the history of the world to ever walk on water, and Peter got to be one of them (Matthew 14:22–36). And as Jesus was feeding over five thousand people on five loaves of bread and two fish, Peter got to participate in passing it out to the people and collecting all the leftovers (John 6:1–15). When the Pharisees called Jesus out for not paying the temple tax, Jesus again asked Peter to participate. Jesus told Peter to go down to the lake, throw in a line, and open the mouth of the first fish he caught. Jesus told him that in the mouth of the fish Peter would find a large silver coin, with which he was to pay the temple tax for both Jesus and himself (Matthew 17:24–27).

In all these instances Jesus did not need to include Peter but chose to let Peter participate. Why? Because *participation leads to passion.* Participation gets you engaged; it strengthens your faith and makes it FUN! Stop and think about how much fun you would have walking down to the fishing dock amongst all the other fishermen, knowing with full confidence that not only were you going to catch a fish but you would pull a large silver coin from its mouth!!! Talk about walking down to the dock with swagger!

Here's the thing: *God doesn't need us to participate, but He wants us to participate.* It's funny how becoming a father has taught me so much about my relationship with God the Father. Currently, my kids are seven (David), five (Makenna), and two (Bella Grace). Any time I'm doing chores or working around the house, the older two kids want to "help." I'll be honest: most of the time I don't want their "help." I know that without their involvement I could complete the task in half the amount of time and do so with greater quality and care. Yet I allow them to participate because I know it's good for them. I know that's how they are going to learn, grow, and mature. Do you see where I'm going with this?

While God doesn't need our "help," He has designed the world in such a way that it benefits from our sloppy, messy, shoddy assistance. Could God do everything without us in a fraction of the time and with greater quality and care? Absolutely. But God encourages and often requires our participation because He knows it's good for us. He knows that's the only way we will learn, grow, and mature.

Mutual Encouragement

The following story is from Jasmine, a former student of mine. I have had the privilege of watching Jasmine learn, grow, and mature spiritually as she has stepped out in faith and participated with God in the lives of friends, family, and neighbors. Jasmine has shared several stories of divine appointments she experienced after reading the *Divine Opportunity* book. This is just one of her many divine encounters to date.

> I'm a resident assistant in the freshmen dorms. I live with and do life with a hall full of freshmen girls here on campus. One particular evening I was doing social rounds, which I really didn't want to be doing. As I was walking down the hallway, I saw this girl, Amairany's, door open. Honestly, I was tired and busy and didn't want to go in, but I felt God saying to me, "Jasmine, people are more important than your to-do list."
>
> As I walked into her room, I got the feeling that her older brother missed her. I didn't know exactly what to make of that, so I asked her, "Do you have an older brother?" She said, "Yeah, I have three brothers. Two older and one younger." I thought about it for a second and said, "Well, I think that God is prompting me to tell you that your older brother misses

you." She said, "Are you sure it's not my younger brother? My two older brothers have been out of the house for a while, and we don't really keep in great touch. But my younger brother I'm closer to and have more of a relationship with." However, I really did feel as though it was her older brother, so I said, "Well, I don't know, but I just felt like it's your older brother and that he misses you." Quickly the conversation moved on, and we eventually said our goodbyes for the night.

Two days later I was walking into the dorm and saw Amairany sitting in the lobby. As she saw me, she jumped up and said, "Oh my goodness, Jasmine, I've got to show you this." She pulled out her phone and said to me, "My mom texted me this picture this morning. It was from my older brother. She said that my second brother was telling her how much he missed me and how proud he was of me for being the first person in our family to go to college." She pulled up this picture on her phone, and it was of her older brother's arm—he had gotten her name, Amairany, tattooed really big across his forearm. Like really big! She said that he'd only had two small tattoos before that, so it wasn't as though he had a sleeve of tattoos that this was hidden in.

I could just tell how impactful this was for her. She is a first-generation college student who is working fulltime, and she really needed this encouragement. Because I took a risk and said what I did two nights earlier, I think she received a double portion of encouragement. First from her brother and his act of support. Second from God working through me in what I shared in advance. That made it more than just brotherly love; it brought in God's love.

The best part about divine appointments is that both people walk away mutually encouraged. It provides a firsthand experience with God for both individuals. Both people walk away with a strengthened and renewed faith in God.

I long to see you so that I may impart to you
some spiritual gift to make you strong—that is,
that you and I may be mutually encouraged by
each other's faith. (Romans 1:11–12)

Jasmine has gone on to share with me several other stories of divine opportunities from just the past year. You'd better believe she is having FUN living out her faith. And on top of that, it's contagious! Everyone around her is encouraged by her stories. The next step of faith for them is to make the move from hearing secondhand stories to living firsthand experiences. The beautiful shift is from hearer to doer (James 1:22). The ripple effects of divine appointments are unlike anything else in our walk of faith.

Firsthand experience with God takes us from partial faith to fullness of faith, from wimpy Christianity to powerful Christianity. Personally, I'm tired of having partial faith; I'm tired of shy, weak, and timid faith. I'm ready for a boldness and power in the name of Jesus Christ! I'm ready for a confident, captivating, and transformative faith. The kind of faith that occurs when you step out into the unknown and experience God's provision.

For the spirit God gave us does not make us timid,
but gives us power, love and self-discipline.
(2 Timothy 1:7)

For the Kingdom of God is not just a lot of talk;
it is living by God's power. (1 Corinthians 4:20 NLT)

The more I've stepped out in faith, the more I've been blown away by the power and faithfulness of God. Before moving on, I want to share one of the most powerful divine appointments of my own. This firsthand experience has helped me realize that there is no limit to what God can accomplish through a willing spirit and a faithful follower who is willing to risk looking dumb for the sake of being obedient.

This divine opportunity includes one of my fellow faculty members and friends, Tom. Tom had the tragic experience of losing his youngest son to depression and suicide a little over a year ago. His son was an eighteen-year-old senior in high school when he took his own life after suffering from depression. As you would expect, Tom and his wife have grieved and mourned the loss of their son. At the time of this divine appointment, Tom had recently passed the one-year anniversary of his son's death and had shared that the second year was actually harder than the first so far. My heart goes out to him, as I can't begin to imagine the pain, suffering, and struggle his family is going through.

It was about a month after the one-year anniversary of the loss of his son that we experienced this divine appointment. One day, before heading off to lunch, I stopped to pray and ask God if there was anyone He had a word for. After sitting in silence for several minutes, trying to clear away all the mental clutter, I finally heard from God. It was then that Tom distinctly came to mind. So I prayed, "God, what is it that you would like Tom to know?" Again I sat in silence, trying to clear away the clutter so that whatever I would share with Tom would be of the Spirit and not of my flesh.

As God began to drop thoughts into my mind, I wrote them down so as not to forget. Most of the thoughts had to do with the loss of his son, his experience of grief, and his willingness to fight the good fight of faith. Then, randomly, an image of a Darth Vader Lego figure came to mind. At first I just thought, "That's weird. Control—Alt—Delete. That's got to be of the flesh." But the image kept coming to mind, to the point at which I couldn't disregard it. So amongst the other notes I wrote: "Is there any significance to a Darth Vader Lego figure?" I still thought this was very awkward and knew it was going to be a hard thing to ask someone in the middle of an otherwise serious conversation about the loss of his son. How are you supposed to have a serious, Spirit-filled time with someone about the loss of their son and then, with a straight face, ask whether there's any significance to a Darth Vader figure?

However, if there is anything I've come to realize in the process of experiencing, researching, writing, and praying about divine appointments, it's that *you'd rather be obedient and be wrong than be disobedient and be right.* So I finished up my notes for Tom and headed out to lunch. On my way back I stopped by Tom's office and I asked if he had time to talk so I could share a few thoughts that had come to mind when I was praying earlier in the day. It ended up being divine timing, as Tom invited me in. He had office hours going on, but no one was showing up.

So I sat down in Tom's office with my pad of notes. To be honest, I was kind of nervous. The loss of a son is so serious and sensitive that I didn't want to over-speak, miss the mark, or hinder his mourning in any way. But I knew Tom would be gracious, and we had an established relationship to the point at which he knew my heart going into this.

I simply prayed, "Holy Spirit, help me." And then I went into it. I told Tom about the prayer time with God before lunch and that he had come to mind and I felt that God had given me these thoughts to share with him. I told Tom I was still very new at hearing from God in this manner, so he could feel free to take or leave what I had to say.

I said, "Tom, I felt like God wanted me to tell you that He is so proud of you for fighting the good fight of faith and not throwing in the towel after the loss of your son. First Timothy 6:12 says, "Fight the good fight of the faith. Take hold of the eternal life to which you were called." 'Cause here's the thing: fights are messy, dirty, and ugly. Fights aren't pretty, choreographed, or for the faint of heart. One way or another, you're getting your hands dirty. God is proud of you for engaging in the process, wrestling back and forth, and fighting the good fight. God loves you and is so proud of you.

"The other thing is that you must always remember that the Bible tells us that the devil is the one that came to steal, kill, and destroy. And the devil, right now, is trying to convince you that it's God who came to steal, kill, and destroy your son.

You must always remember that it's the devil who came to steal, kill, and destroy, and it's God who came to give life and give it abundantly. Don't let the devil do harm and blame-shift that responsibility to God. There is no greater trick that the devil can do than to steal, kill, and destroy within your very own family and then convince you that it was God who did so."

Then I got to that strange question I had written down. I thought to myself, "I can't believe I'm about to ask this." I said to Tom, "This next question may seem a bit weird, but I'm just going to ask: Is there any significance to a Darth Vader Lego figure?" Tom immediately said "Yes!" I replied, "Really!?!" I was shocked, quite frankly. Tom went on, "There's a story behind that." Again, I said, "Really!?!" Tom replied, "Yeah" before he stood up, walked over to a bookshelf that was off to the side in his office, reached up on top, and pulled down a Darth Vader figure!!! My heart stopped and I thought, "You've got to be kidding me!"

Tom set this Darth Vader figure on the desk in front of me, and I read the inscription at the bottom of the figure: "Galaxy's Best Father." Tom said, "This was a Father's Day present my son gave me when he was eight years old." I was speechless. Then Tom's face lit up, with more joy than I had ever seen in his eyes, as he told me the story behind the Darth Vader. He said, "My boys always liked watching *Star Wars* growing up. We would watch the movies together. There was one particular time I snuck up behind my son and said, "Michael, I am your Father!" He would joke that I was Darth Dad. So it was a wonderful memory and Father's Day gift, and I've saved it ever since. And as for the Lego part, Michael's favorite thing growing up was playing with Legos. He would make these amazing Lego creations, just using his imagination. Michael wanted to work for Lego when he got older."

I still couldn't believe it. It blew my mind that God could put this man into my prayers, give me thoughts to share with him, and give Tom the special reminder of such a wonderful memory with his son through something as random as a

Darth Vader figure. I just thanked God for the word for Tom and for giving me the courage to actually ask about this Darth Vader. I realized that if I hadn't been obedient with the Darth Vader thought, we both would have missed out on this powerful, faith-building, firsthand experience with God.

Tom went on to confirm the previous thoughts I had shared with him and how much it meant to him that I would take the time to share all that. To finish up, I prayed over Tom and asked God to continue to speak to him through this difficult season.

The next morning I was back in my office praying again and thanking God for this ridiculously amazing divine appointment when He dropped another thought into my prayer. There was more significance to the Darth Vader figure than just hearing Tom's Father's Day story and seeing the joy in his face over the fond memory. God had more to say to Tom through this Darth Vader figure. So I wrote down several more thoughts and dropped back by his office again.

I told Tom, "I think there was more God wanted to reveal to you about the Darth Vader Father's Day present. God wants you to know that He was with you that day, as He has been every day. God wants you to know that you're still the same father today as you were the day you received the Darth Vader—Galaxy's Best Father! The devil is trying to convince you that God is the one who came to steal, kill, and destroy, AND he's trying to convince you that you're a bad father and that God is a bad Father. This is a big fat ugly LIE. You absolutely MUST hang on to the truth. Take captive every negative thought and teach it to obey Christ. You're still the same father today as you were the day you received the Darth Vader Galaxy's Best Dad. God is still the same Father today as He was the day you received the Darth Vader. God is the same yesterday, today, and forever."

One of the things with which Tom struggled most was the fact that he had gone to work the day his son took his own life. On the day of the suicide Michael had gotten ready and headed off to school, so Tom had thought he must have been okay. Tom then went off to work. What he didn't realize was that after he left, Michael had circled back around to the house—and that's when he had taken his life. Since then, Tom has carried a lot of guilt about going to work that day and has blamed himself for not having been there and done more.

I continued, "Let me give you an example, Tom. While I'm at work today, if my son were to come home from school and go running across the street to play with his friends and didn't look both ways and got hit by a car and died, would that change who I am as a father? Would that make me a bad dad?" Tom replied, "Of course not!" I said, "The same is true for you! I know it's hard to see that from your perspective, but it's the truth! Just because your son suffered from depression and his life was lost while you were at work does not change who you are as a father!!!

"The changing circumstances of this world don't change who God is. He's the same yesterday, today, and forever. So are you! You're still the son of a living God, and that never changes, regardless of your circumstances. It's okay to grieve—God is grieving with you! But He's not just a co-griever, He's the Great Comforter! Take comfort, my friend! The Great Comforter has given us both such an incredible token of His love through the Darth Vader figure. God is with you and for you! He loves you, and He's proud of you!"

> Since the day we heard about you, we have not stopped praying for you . . . that you may live a life worthy of the Lord and please him in every way. (Colossians 1:9–10)

> We constantly pray for you, that our God may make you worthy of his calling, and that by his power he may bring to fruition your every desire for goodness and your every deed prompted by faith. We pray this so that the name of our Lord Jesus may be glorified in you, and you in him, according to the grace of our God and the Lord Jesus Christ. (2 Thessalonians 1:11–12)

DISCUSSION QUESTIONS

1. How would you rate Christianity as an overall faith, in terms of being fun, on a scale of 1 to 10, 1 being extremely boring and 10 being extremely fun? What stories from Scripture are examples of the potential for fun in Christianity?

2. How would you rate your personal testimony on a scale of 1 to 10—1 being extremely boring and 10 being extremely exciting? What are three things you're praying to experience to grow your faith and add excitement to your testimony? What do you need to step out and do to put yourself in a position to experience those things?

3. When it comes to playing the game of faith, are you a starter or a benchwarmer? Are you playing or watching? Are you in the game or in the stands? What are three things you could do in this season of life to increase your participation? Examples might include volunteering at church; joining or leading a life group; volunteering in a service project in your community; praying with family members, friends, co-workers, or neighbors for a needed miracle; praying for your enemies; extending radical generosity; extending radical grace and forgiveness; or extending radically polite manners to people at work or while running errands, etc.

Good Soil and Ripe Harvest

"You intended to harm me, but God intended
it for good to accomplish what is now being
done, the saving of many lives."
—Genesis 50:20

A footnote in the Jesus-Centered Bible (NLT) states, "Genesis 50:20—
Here Joseph reveals something central to the heart of Jesus: He makes
beautiful things out of ugly things. He takes harmful motivations and
weaves something redemptive in their midst (Romans 8:28)." I believe
this is what we are seeing in modern culture right now with a storm
passing through, largely made up of busyness and technology addictions
that leave people moody, in ever-increasing need of "me-time," and
treating others as an inconvenience rather than an opportunity.
This storm is leaving in its path isolation, depression, anxiety, and
disconnection, as never before. Yet I know God will make beautiful
things out of ugly things. He will take harmful motivations and weave
something redemptive in their midst. *As this storm passes through, I see it
leaving behind an incredibly fertile soil and ripe harvest.*

In this information age, we suffer from information overload. In this opinion age, we experience opinion overload. In this technology age, we struggle with technology overload. Our generation gets voices coming at us from every angle, at all times of day, and with every type of perspective. *This has resulted in a schizophrenic generation, a people with too many voices vying for attention in their heads and no sense of the real, authentic voice.* On a positive note, the crazier things get, the hungrier people are for truth. And the good news we bring is the only stable, reliable, unchanging, unwavering Truth of Christ that has stood the test of time for over two thousand years. As Christ said, "I am the way and the truth and the life" (John 14:6).

While the storm has done its damage, it has managed to leave behind a remnant of fertile soil and a ripe harvest. I'm telling you, it is easier to have a divine appointment now than it ever has been. In big cities, especially, people have grown so accustomed to silent commuter trains, lines of phone gazers, and nearly complete avoidance and lack of acknowledgment from strangers. Because of that, basic manners are now WOWing and can be turned into conversation starters. People are now impressed by the littlest things, like holding a door open and waiting for someone behind you, introducing yourself to the person in front or behind you in line, asking how someone is doing and genuinely caring about their answer, maintaining eye contact with your conversational partner rather than constantly checking your phone, or recalling someone's name and using it in conversation. It's fertile soil for divine opportunities, and it's a ripe harvest for those who are desperate and ready for connection.

"The seed falling on good soil refers to someone who hears the word and understands it. This is the one who produces a crop, yielding a hundred, sixty or thirty times what was sown." (Matthew 13:23)

In this chapter I'm going to give you several examples of how *the storm has prepared the way by leaving behind people of good soil that is fertile and ready for truth, love, grace, and connection.* Amidst the storm are counterfeit truth, love, grace, and connection. But coming out of the storm is longing for the real thing. If you are faithful to plant seeds, you will see a harvest of thirty, sixty, or even a hundred times as much as has been planted.

The Good Soil

Evelyn, a customer service representative for a financial center, shared the following story of planting a simple seed of care and concern and then seeing immediate growth.

A customer showed up recently who looked very sad and somewhat desperate. As I was helping her with her payment, I was feeling the need to ask how she was doing. Initially, I was a little hesitant to ask her if she was okay, because I didn't think it was my place to ask, given that we were total strangers in a professional setting handling her transaction. But we got to a point where I was waiting on something to process before we could proceed, so I decided to ask her how she was doing and what was going on.

When I asked how she was doing, she immediately broke down. She said that her mother had passed away a month earlier and that not a single person had asked her how she was doing until that moment. I teared up as she told me her story.

This woman was about forty years old, and her mother had been about sixty. Her mother had been diagnosed with cancer and was receiving treatment. The treatment had been having a positive effect and seemed to be moving along well. The doctors had even said that her mother was improving. But then, quickly and unexpectedly, her mother's condition had gotten worse, and in a short turn of events she had passed away.

This poor woman was so torn up over the situation, yet no one in her life had bothered to ask her about it, let alone comfort her through it. She said that she really appreciated my asking her about how she was feeling because she was feeling horrible and felt worse when no one had followed up with her after her mother's death.

Then she began to tell me to love my mom and spend time with her because things happen very unexpectedly. We talked for a few minutes as I comforted her over the loss of her mom and as she inspired me to spend more time with and pay more attention to my mom. Then she said thank you again, because our short conversation had made her feel better. As I look back on that conversation, I realize that this had been a divine opportunity, and it had felt really good to be there for that woman in her time of need.

It's remarkable that in the age of digital connection there is so little genuine connection. All it takes is someone who is mindful of those around them and compassionate enough to connect in a heartfelt way. There is so much fertile soil; it's just a matter of planting seeds. Another example once again involved my father-in-law, David Watson.

This divine appointment happened the weekend of the book launch for *Divine Opportunity*. We had celebrated the launch with a party on Saturday afternoon, which several family members had come into town for. The next day we decided to take our family to Newport Beach to hang out. It just so happened that both my father and my father-in-law had worn their matching Divine Opportunity t-shirts to the beach that day. The t-shirts have the Divine Opportunity logo on the front, which has a DO with a small cross inside the O.

At one point during the day, the dads took off separately, walking around the Newport pier to soak in the sites and look out over the ocean. It just so happened that there was a young family touring the pier at the same time. It was a husband, wife, and two kids. This family first walked past my dad and just happened to notice his DO shirt. At first they didn't think too much of it, until a couple of minutes later they saw my father-in-law wearing the same shirt.

The wife stopped him and commented, "We saw another guy walking around here a couple minutes ago wearing the same shirt. What's the deal? What does the DO stand for?" My father-in-law, David, replied, "It's stands for Divine Opportunity." The wife responded, "What's a divine opportunity?" David explained, "A divine opportunity is when God brings two or more people together to deliver a message through one person to another." To which the wife asked, "Well then, what's the message?" David took a deep breath to hear from the Holy Spirit and replied, "Well, I think the message is that God knows exactly what you are going through right now and wants you to know that you're not going through it alone. He is going through it with you. He loves you and will see you through it."

The wife immediately began to cry. She leaned into her husband's arms, thanked David for the message, and began to walk off with the family. The couple never said what they were going through or what the circumstances were, but clearly God had touched their hearts right there on the Newport pier. Whatever the couple had experienced, this short interaction left them standing in fertile soil, and a beautiful seed of God's mercy was planted and watered that day. All it took was a simple inquiry about a shirt, with a simple response about the hope and glory of God. All that was required to connect the inquiry with the response was a faithful servant willing to give this couple an opportunity to experience God.

The Harvest Is Ripe

> "Don't you have a saying, 'It's still four months until harvest'? I tell you, open your eyes and look at the fields! They are ripe for harvest. Even now the one who reaps draws a wage and harvests a crop for eternal life, so that the sower and the reaper may be glad together. Thus the saying 'One sows and another reaps' is true. I sent you to reap what you have not worked for. Others have done the hard work, and you have reaped the benefits of their labor." (John 4:35–38)

> He who gathers crops in summer is a prudent son,
> but he who sleeps during harvest is a disgraceful
> son. (Proverbs 10:5)

My wife and I have a tangerine tree in our backyard, and this thing produces some serious tangerines; we're talking hundreds. This past spring was our first year at this new house with this tree, and we greatly underestimated the harvest. There were so many fresh tangerines that we weren't able to give enough away. We ate many ourselves, we gave lots away to neighbors, and anyone who came over we would load up with a bagful to take home. Even after all those efforts to harvest this tangerine tree, we still reached the end of the season with a good deal of rotting fruit lying on the ground. At one point I looked into this tree, only to see so much wasted rotting fruit that we never got to, and God convicted me by saying, "This is what just your neighborhood of souls looks like, let alone the city, state, nation, or world. The harvest is ripe, but the workers are few. Wake up! For it is disgraceful to sleep through the harvest." There is so much ripe, low-hanging fruit that is easily harvested with minimal effort."

> Another personal experiences of my own came from this past summer, my wife and I went on a couples' trip to Palm Springs and experienced a wonderful divine appointment over the weekend. We went away with five other couples and zero kids. It was amazing; I get all excited just thinking about it again right now. Not the divine appointment, but the fact that there were zero kids. Although the divine appointment was pretty cool, too.
>
> In all seriousness, we were in Palm Springs with our friends for about two-and-a-half days. On Saturday of this weekend trip, we decided to go see a movie matinée showing at around 2:00 p.m. You might be thinking, "Wow, you all were really cutting loose and getting crazy on your vacation." But when you have three kids ages seven and under, getting to see a movie on your own is a real treat.

So all six of us couples headed out to the movie. We got our tickets and snacks and headed into the theater. As we walked in, there was only one guy in the entire place, a super muscular African-American guy in his lower thirties, looking rather trendy with camo pants and a cut off shirt, which really complimented his massive biceps and cool looking tattoos that ran up and down his arms. Being the first one there, he had taken the prime seat, three-quarters of the way back and right in the middle.

Four of the couples walked in ahead of us and sat down a couple of rows ahead of this guy. My wife and I followed behind another couple (all four of us are white and in our upper thirties), and the husband decided to walk around and go into the aisle right ahead of this African-American guy, taking the seat directly in front of him. So picture this: an entirely empty theater except for one guy, and our friend chooses the one seat directly in front of him. He didn't even have his tiny wife sit there but sat there himself with his big self and giant dome. I was watching this whole thing unfold as I trailed behind him with my wife, Debra. I couldn't help but point out the hilarity in my friend's seat selection to my wife before I headed off to the restroom.

While I walked out, the rest of them settled into the seats right in front of this guy. Debra said hi and made a joke of the seat selection to break the ice. But when she did, the guy took it well and they all began to talk. By the time I came back from the restroom, the four of them were mid-conversation as though they were all old friends. The super muscular guy's name was Eric, and he was opening up about his lady and kids. He said that she had taken them to an audition, so he came to see a movie while he had a couple of hours to kill. As he continued to talk about his kids, he shared with us how he was raising them to develop a good work ethic, earn what they got, and treat people with respect. He was so passionate and motivated as he spoke.

I was seated the furthest away from him, and the commercials playing in the background were quite loud, so I could barely hear what he was saying. But I picked up on how passionate and motivated he was. Whatever he was selling, I was buying. This guy was getting me all pumped up to go back home and be a better dad to my own kids. So as the movie started to come on, I asked him if he did any motivational speaking. He said he had done a little, but not much. I told him that he needed to think about doing more of it because he had a gift. Then we quickly traded business cards. Turns out Eric was a personal trainer, which I probably could have gathered from the size of his biceps; the business card just stated the obvious at this point.

But the movie started and our conversation abruptly came to a close. All throughout the movie, I kept sensing this prompting that I needed to encourage Eric after the movie to really press into his motivational gifting. I sensed that God wanted to encourage Eric and lift him up. To be honest, this ruined the movie for me because I was thinking about how I would be able to approach him. Here we were in a loud movie theater, by this point there were more people in the room, and it was going to be a challenge to have a personal moment with him before he walked out.

As the movie came to a close, I was on the edge of my seat, ready to pounce on this guy and figure out what God had in store. Sure enough, the second the movie ended Eric jumped up, patted me on the shoulder, and said, "Nice to meet you all. Have a great weekend." I quickly replied, "Eric, can I talk to you in the hallway for a minute?" He looked at me as though a teacher had just caught him red-handed and asked him to step outside the room. To be honest, that's kind of how I felt, too. It's awkward to call someone out into the hallway of a movie theater, but I knew that was the only chance I would have to share a word with him.

Thank God, Eric was cool with it, and we headed outside the room. Then I shared with him what God had put on my heart about his motivational gifting. I said, "Man, Eric, I got to tell you, you really need to take this motivational gifting seriously. I felt so inspired by just the few things you shared with us before the movie. I believe that God has a motivational anointing on your life and a gift for inspiring people. Have you thought about pushing into that more?"

Eric and I ended up talking back and forth for a few minutes about his current jobs, his family, and what direction in life he was headed. He talked about his passion for working with young athletes in Palm Springs and training them up as young men, not just as football players. It was fun to hear more about his passions. While it was a special moment, I didn't quite feel as though it had the impact I had been hoping it would.

As things leveled off in conversation, I asked Eric if we could pray for him before he left. After his saying yes, we headed down to the lobby of the movie theater to find my wife and our friends, Ryan and Jill and Steve and Katie. I told them we were going to pray over Eric, who said he would like prayer for his family and for his mom and sister, who'd had a really rough go of things in their lives.

So here's the scene in this movie theater in Palm Springs—a big, muscular African-American and three white couples who were huddled around him, laying hands on him to pray as he bowed his head in the center of the group. And I all out went for it in prayer. I lifted him up in Jesus' name, praying for him, his career, his motivational gifting, his lady and kids, his mom and sister—all while my wife and friends were praying, giving Amens throughout, until I closed out this full prayer in Jesus' name.

The six of us then stepped back from Eric as he brought his head back up, and I looked at him and saw these big streams of tears pouring down his face. Which I was not at all expecting.

Eric was fully choked up and had to take a minute to regain his emotions before he could talk. When he had finally composed himself, he shared how much it had meant to him that six white people had taken the time to talk with him, care for him, and pray over him.

What I didn't realize was that when I had left to use the restroom and my wife had broken the ice by joking about our friend sitting directly in front of him, Eric had said that he actually appreciated the fact that we sat so close to him. While I was in the restroom, Eric had shared with them that often when he is in a theater or restaurant and white people come in, they tend to sit away from him. In fact, just a few days earlier he and a friend had been in Panda Express, and at the beginning of their meal they were the only two in the restaurant. Then a white couple came in and sat on the other side of the restaurant. As others came in, they sat on the side with the white couple. Eric said that by the time he and his friend left, the restaurant felt lopsided.

Eric shared that when we came into the theater and sat directly in front of him, he appreciated it. When we took the time to talk with him before the movie, he was all the more grateful. When I shared my encouragement with him in the hallway, he was moved. But when we all huddled around him and prayed for him, it was overwhelming. You could tell that Eric had some serious racial wounds that he carried with him. And what I thought was a divine opportunity to encourage his motivational gifting turned out to be God doing some racial reconciliation. It was as though a racial wound had been healed up. By the end of this whole thing, we were all teared up and blown away by what God had done in that one trip to the movies. I have since kept in touch with Eric, and I continue to reach out to him with encouragement and support. I'm excited to see what God is doing in his life.

I would never have imagined that simply having six white people offer some kindness, care, and prayer over this man could have made that kind of impact. It's further evidence that this perfect storm has left behind a very ripe harvest. With the media fanning the flame of racial division, there is fertile soil and ripe harvest ready for reconciliation. Let's spend less time bantering online about the problem and more time engaged in the solution. *The solution is to be doers of God's Word, not just hearers.* Being doers of God's Word means engaging in divine opportunities with ALL God's people. *You'll be surprised how much ripe fruit is within arm's reach.*

> Farmers who wait for perfect weather never plant.
> If they watch every cloud, they never harvest.
> (Ecclesiastes 11:4 NLT)

This next divine opportunity comes from Alyssa, a student life professional, who reflected upon a divine appointment from her days in graduate school. It was when she was surrounded by skeptics that she encountered good soil disguised as dry soil.

I went to a Christian university for my undergraduate degree, and it was a great place for growing in my faith. It was like being in a bubble where everyone believes the same thing as you and you're allowed and encouraged to grow. It was great for my faith development. But because of that I didn't receive a lot of pushback on my faith until I graduated and went to grad school. It was in grad school that I was in an environment with people who didn't appreciate Christianity and really questioned why I believed. They felt that Christianity wasn't inclusive in certain ways and aspects. My first semester was my hardest, because it was filled with people constantly questioning what I believed and why I believed it. I felt like I was regularly on the defensive. It didn't seem like these people were coming to me seeking to understand, but rather coming at me with questions, ready to debate and attack.

In particular, there was one of my cohort members, Andy, who would regularly want to meet up and talk. We would have hour-long discussions about things that came up in class and about my faith and about God. He would ask why I believed. I remember him saying that Christians seemed like blind followers, like sheep. I remember him just asking me to tell him why this thing was even real.

Initially, I saw it as an opportunity to share my faith, but then over time I felt like the conversation wasn't going anywhere. Like there were walls up, and I wasn't at all being heard. So I started to put my walls up, too.

Having been in an environment where faith wasn't talked well about at all in the classroom, and feeling like Andy was so closed off, I began to disengage. I remember going home in tears and calling my parents, asking, "Why am I even here?" It was such a contrasting experience from going to a Christian undergraduate university to being at a public university. The people I interacted with in grad school were skeptical of my Christian faith, and constantly questioning my beliefs. But I was thankful for my undergraduate experience so that I could articulate my faith and be better prepared to take on those questions.

After those conversations with Andy, we both eventually realized that this wasn't going anywhere and retreated from those discussions. We were still friends, and there weren't any hard feelings. We were in this small cohort of about twenty students, so we would see each other all the time—we just knew not to go there anymore.

It was my last semester of a two-year program, so about a year-and-a-half later, when Andy finally circled back around to this conversation. It was then that he asked me to grab lunch, and the invitation had a similar vibe to the original invitations where he would grill me with questions about my faith. I just thought, "Oh, here we go again."

As we met up for lunch, he opened by saying that he actually wanted to share his past experience with me. As he got into it, Andy shared that he had grown up in the church and had actually been a youth leader. He said he could quote

Scripture just like anyone else in the church. Back in high school he had been that person who was helping others grow in their faith. At this point my jaw just dropped, because based on the questions in our original conversations you would never have thought he'd had any relationship with Christ or even knew much about Christianity.

But here he was saying that he had grown up in the church, knew Scripture, and had been a youth leader. Andy shared that when he went off to college he had started questioning God and even His very existence. He shared that he had grown away from his faith and by that time described himself as an atheist.

"The reason I poked and prodded and asked those questions was because"—and I'll never forget this—"I was hoping that something you would say would be something I could hang on to for myself." He wanted to know why I believed because he was hoping that something I said would spark something inside him to believe again as well.

Then he proceeded to tell me, "I just want you to know that I've started going back to church. I've been dating this girl who is a Christian for a little while now, and she has brought me back to church, and I've been pressing into God again. Before we leave this time together, I just want you to know that God is doing something in my life."

That was completely unexpected. I couldn't believe it!

What I learned from this is that you never know how God is using you. Even when it hurts and you feel alone and attacked, God is doing something, is planting seeds through you and others. But I do look back on that experience and see it as both a divine opportunity and a missed opportunity, because, I think, had I not backed away and retreated, I could have been more a part of Andy's experience and journey than I was.

People are craving understanding of and experience with God. Their line of questioning and approach may not always indicate that, but so many are, and they are just hoping that something you say about your faith and reason for belief will be something they can hang on to for themselves.

Even if you should suffer for what is right, you are blessed. "Do not fear their threats; do not be frightened. But in your hearts revere Christ as Lord. *Always be prepared to give an answer to everyone who asks you to give the reason for the hope that you have. But do this with gentleness and respect,* keeping a clear conscience, so that those who speak maliciously against your good behavior in Christ may be ashamed of their slander. For it is better, if it is God's will, to suffer for doing good than for doing evil. (1 Peter 3:14–17, emphasis added)

Are you ready to give an account for the hope you have as a believer? Are you prepared to do so in a gentle and respectful way? And keep it gentle and respectful regardless of their line of questioning, inquiring, or attacking your source of hope? Busyness, technology addictions, and increased loneliness and depression have led to an extremely fertile soil and ripe harvest. Are you ready to plant seeds, water others, and harvest that which God has already grown and ripened?

DISCUSSION QUESTIONS

1. If someone were to look at your life, would they see enough fruit—love, joy, peace, patience, kindness, and self-control—to ask about it? And if someone were to ask you where your hope and joy come from, how would you respond? Practice what you would actually say.

2. Where in your past have you left behind a ripe harvest that you did not take the time to go after? What can you do differently during this season of life to avoid missing similar opportunities? For example, past neighbors, co-workers, classmates, teammates, or friends you had a relationship with but never took the time to speak with about their relationship with God.

3. Busyness, technology addictions, and increased loneliness have led to extremely fertile soil and a ripe harvest. Are you ready to plant seeds, water others, and harvest that which God has already grown and ripened? What are some practical steps you could take in the next week to plant a seed of hope in someone's life—watering a seed by encouraging or checking in with someone you know is still on the fence about faith—harvesting fruit by asking the hard questions of someone you have been procrastinating and delaying going after?

YOU Are the Answer to Prayer

> For we are God's handiwork, created in Christ
> Jesus to do good works, which God prepared
> in advance for us to do.
> —Ephesians 2:10

> Each of us did the work the Lord gave us. I planted the
> seed in your hearts, and Apollos watered it, but it was
> God who made it grow. It's not important who does the
> planting, or who does the watering. What's important
> is that God makes the seed grow. The one who plants
> and the one who waters work together with the same
> purpose. And both will be rewarded for their own hard
> work. For we are both God's workers. And you are
> God's field. You are God's building.
> —1 Corinthians 3:5–9 NLT

Whereas the NLT says that we are "God's workers," the ESV states, "For we are God's fellow workers." Stop and think about this for a moment. We are God's fellow workers!!! The same God who spoke the world into existence wants to partner with you to bring about good works! God could speak those same good works into existence, but instead He wants to use you to bring them into being. That's insanely awesome!

Let's be real: Christianity is a team sport! It's the body of Christ that makes up the team. And God wants no one to be a benchwarmer, He wants all to be involved, active, and participative. As stated before, participation leads to passion, and *God wants to set you afire with passion that burns for loving people and engaging people with the heart of Christ.*

Paul says it's not important *who* does the planting or *who* does the watering. I interpret that to mean that *it is important that someone* does the planting and *someone* does the watering. If Paul and Apollos had not planted seeds or watered them, there would have been nothing for God to grow. We need to take action and give God a chance! We need more people planting and more people watering. The more we plant and the more we water the more God has to grow. The lack of growth is certainly not because of a lack of need, and it's certainly not because of a lack of God. It's because of a lack of "someones" who are failing to do the planting and watering. (You can read in chapter 11 of *Divine Opportunity* an elaboration on what it looks like to plant, water, and grow.)

Let me give you an example. This missed opportunity comes from a friend of mine, Kelsey, who missed a chance to speak into her friend's life during a crucial season. This is not to throw Kelsey under the bus for her disobedience, as I can guarantee we have all been in her position more times than we would like to admit. And Kelsey has also had wonderfully amazing divine opportunities as well, one of hers appearing in the *Divine Opportunity* book. However, this missed opportunity will raise awareness of our lack of planting and watering.

> I had a roommate in college whom I lived with for two years. When I met her, she was a new believer who wasn't very deep in her faith and didn't live as though the Lord were in charge of her life. Over the course of the two years of my living with her, she grew in her faith a lot and was pursuing the Lord and loving Him. She had changed her life for God and wanted to be used by Him. However, during this season she was dating

my good friend for four years and was pushing very hard to get married. The guy kept telling her that he didn't feel that the Lord had told him he was ready for marriage and that he felt very clearly that if the time were right and God wanted him to propose, he would know. She was very persistent and pushy and made comments like, "Well, you're not close to the Lord right now, so you can't really hear what He's telling you."

Fast-forward to spring break of my sophomore year, which would have been her senior year. At this point we were really close. But she had decided to go to California for spring break without her boyfriend because he had a basketball tournament that week and couldn't travel. While she was in California she met this guy and started talking to him and hung out with him a lot that week. She came home and was texting with him while she was still dating my friend. I remember having an initial conversation, just sharing that I was leery about this. I was praying with her and serving as an accountability partner to her. I remember that she didn't want it—it was like, maybe, two days after she had gotten back that we had this conversation. She didn't respond positively and acted as though she was having fun and was tired of waiting to get married.

I saw her for only three days that next week while she finished her internship and was going home for the summer— or so she said. *Over this period I kept feeling as though the Lord were prompting me to continue to press the issue and to speak truth into her life about what He wanted for her, even though she probably already knew.* It was as though God were saying, "You need to be her accountability partner because everyone else is going to ignore this. Her family is broken, and everyone else in her life tells her to do what feels good."

But yet I didn't. I didn't talk to her about it because I was close to the guy she was dating and didn't want to be in the middle. I didn't want to have to be the one to tell him. He had been at nationals for basketball at the time and had purchased a ring to propose to her when he came home from that tournament. In actuality, he came home and she told him, before leaving, that there was another guy. I didn't see her and found out from him that she had broken up with him.

Then she left for the summer and moved to California, and within months of being there she got pregnant. As a result, she felt forced to marry him and moved further down in this unhealthy direction. We didn't speak. She didn't call me, and when I would call her she wouldn't call me back. I just remember feeling like, "God, she's really lost . . . really lost." I missed my chance to be her friend and to walk alongside her through the process; instead, I was hoping that someone else would do it.

Just recently, I was in California, and she still lived out there. She had been married for about four years to this guy, and I knew nothing about him. She'd actually had a miscarriage so never had the baby. When I saw her, she shared that he had cheated on her and had never been a good husband. *She had known the whole time that it had been a mistake, but she said that no one had really said anything to her, so she had just gone with it.* But it was cool because God had taken this full circle. She had gotten really involved with a church and was feeling back on the right track. *I just think there was a lot of heartache that could have been avoided if I hadn't taken the path of least resistance.* She went through really bad heartache and even walked away from the Lord for a couple of years.

Think about these two statements from Kelsey: "She had known the whole time it had been a mistake, but she said that no one had really said anything to her, so she had just gone with it," and "I just think there was a lot of heartache that could have been avoided if I hadn't taken the path of least resistance." Think about that on a grander scale across the globe. Think about the heartache that could be avoided if we, as Christians, didn't take the path of least resistance. Think about what our communities, cities, states, and nations would look like if we were to transform all the potentially missed opportunities into divine appointments—perhaps even if we did so with half of these opportunities. Think about the prayers that could be answered, the lives that could be touched, and the transformation that could take place.

Why Didn't God Answer Our Prayers?

The truth is, I'm tired of hearing people ask these same old questions over and over: "Why didn't God answer our prayers? Why didn't God intervene?" It's crazy to think of all the times we unjustly blame God for the seemingly unanswered prayers in life, as though God were cruelly withholding Himself from our lives.

Recently, I was convicted by the thought, "What if I were the answer to someone else's prayer? What if someone else's prayer went unanswered because of my disobedience? Not because of God. Perhaps God desired to answer their prayers and was willing to do so through me, not through the snap of His fingers. *It's not God who is cruelly withholding Himself from people's lives; it's we Christians who are the cruel ones withholding ourselves and Christ from people's lives.*"

Up until that moment, I had always thought my disobedience was just between me and God. That my disobedience was just something I struggled with, was ashamed of, and that it impacted only the relationship between me and God. It was in this moment that I realized that my disobedience isn't just between me and God but impacts other people. My disobedience is not a fundamentally neutral act. Let me say that again and include all of us: *our disobedience is not a neutral act; other people's lives are negatively impacted by our disobedience.*

In fact, our actions are weighted in ways that we can't possibly know in the moment—but God does, and that's why He is prompting us to act, to trust, to engage. Think about this for a moment: our actions are weighted in ways we can't possibly know. This means that a short but heartfelt conversation could have either little impact or tremendous impact. There is no way of knowing the full scope and impact of any given connection. *All we can do is seek to bless and release. Bless others with love, care, and prayer. Then release both them and the results into the hands of our heavenly Father.*

> Plant your seed in the morning and keep busy all afternoon, for you don't know if profit will come from one activity or another—or maybe both. (Ecclesiastes 11:6)

When you fully realize that you are an outlet of God's goodness to people, then the idea of withholding that goodness from others seems cruel. And believe it or not, it often takes very little time and effort to be a conduit of God's love. You have to take action in order to be an outlet for God's goodness; you cannot be passive and disengaged and be a Christian, plain and simple. A man once said to me, "My friend is a really devoted Christian." I thought to myself, "Is there any other kind?" If we are true believers in Christ and lovingly devoted to Him, then, logically, this has to produce obedience in action. As Jesus said in John 14:21, "Whoever has my commands and keeps them is the one who loves me."

One of the most motivating things I have ever heard came from Kathie Lee Gifford from the *Today Show*. In an interview with Megyn Kelly on *Today*, Kathie Lee was asked why she was always so outspoken about her faith, and I was called out in conviction by the Holy Spirit in her response:

> If you had the cure for cancer, would you keep it to yourself, or would you share it with others? You'd share it with others! The thing is, I believe that I have the cure for cancer of the soul, and His name is Jesus. And you better believe I'm going to share it with everyone I can.

That statement really woke me up to the reality of Christ and the calling of the Great Commission—to go and give others an opportunity to experience God.

Ananias, the Answer to Prayer

To make the point that we very well could be the answer to other people's prayers, I want to take a look at the single greatest conversion story in the history of the world. In Acts 9 we read about Saul, the most notorious persecutor of the early Christians. This man Saul was a bad dude, not to be messed with. He had it out for any and all followers of the Way—Jesus Christ. He wanted every last follower of the Way brought back to Jerusalem in chains and punished severely, if not killed, for no other reason than that they believed Jesus was the Savior of the world. And Saul was good at his job—until . . .

As he neared Damascus on his journey, suddenly a light from heaven flashed around him He fell to the ground and heard a voice say to him, "Saul, Saul, why do you persecute me?"

"Who are you, Lord?" Saul asked.

"I am Jesus, whom you are persecuting," he replied. "Now get up and go into the city, and you will be told what you must do."

The men traveling with Saul stood there speechless; they heard the sound but did not see anyone. Saul got up from the ground, but when he opened his eyes he could see nothing. So they led him by the hand into Damascus. For three days he was blind, and did not eat or drink anything.

In Damascus there was a disciple named Ananias. The Lord called to him in a vision, "Ananias!"

Yes, Lord," he answered.

The Lord told him, "*Go to the house of Judas on Straight Street and ask for a man from Tarsus named Saul, for he is praying. In a vision he has seen a man named Ananias come and place his hands on him to restore his sight.*"

"Lord," Ananias answered, "I have heard many reports about this man and all the harm he has done to your holy people in Jerusalem. And he has come here with authority from the chief priests to arrest all who call on your name."

But the Lord said to Ananias, "Go! This man is my chosen instrument to proclaim my name to the Gentiles and their kings and to the people of Israel. I will show him how much he must suffer for my name."

Then Ananias went to the house and entered it. Placing his hands on Saul, he said, "Brother Saul, the Lord—Jesus, who appeared to you on the road as you were coming here—has sent me so that you may see again and be filled with the Holy Spirit." Immediately, something like scales fell from Saul's eyes, and he could see again. He got up and was baptized, and after taking some food, he regained his strength. (Acts 9:3–19, emphasis added)

Make sure you catch the italicized portion, especially "for he is praying." God essentially says to Ananias, "You, Ananias, are the answer to that prayer. You will lay hands on Saul, and he will be healed." This is CRAZY! God struck Saul with instant blindness. He could have instantly cured Saul of his blindness, but He chose to use Ananias as His fellow worker, God's representative, to provide the answer to Saul's prayer. And then Saul became Paul, God's chosen instrument to take His message to the Gentiles and to kings, as well as to the people of Israel.

As my friend Julian put it: "Think about how many Sauls are walking around this planet who may never become Pauls, because their Ananias is disengaged, distracted, and disobedient to the Lord God Almighty."

Never treat a divine assignment lightly. God has legions of angels anxious to do His bidding yet He asks YOU to do it! (Richard Blackaby)

Stop for one minute and consider some things that have not come into existence in your life or others' lives. Consider the times you've heard people express frustrations over their unanswered prayers. Could it be that the things that have not yet come into existence were because of your disobedience and inaction and the fact that you never even gave God a chance?

Think about the people praying for revival to break out in their community, yet no one goes out and shares the gospel, no one goes out and talks about Jesus, no one steps out to pray for healing, and no one even gives God a chance to spark a revival. A revival isn't just going to break out while you're at the coffee shop talking about the Kardashians. You've got to talk about Jesus. No one is going to get healed while you're at home watching reruns of *Chicago Med*. You've got to go lay hands on people and pray with all your might. No one is going to experience the supernatural while you're sitting around watching YouTube videos. You've got to go out, start conversations, listen to people's stories, and bring God into their source of pain.

Somewhere right now there are parents praying desperately for their child who is suffering from depression and loneliness. These parents are praying that God would intervene in the midst of their child's pain—and you might be the answer to that prayer. Somewhere right now there are children praying desperately for their parents who bicker and argue nonstop. These children are praying that God would send someone to intervene in their marriage and turn their hearts back to God and to each other—and you might be the answer to that prayer.

Somewhere right now there is someone praying for their roommate who is about to walk away from their faith and leave the church for good. This roommate himself is praying that God would send someone older, wiser, and more spiritually mature to intervene and answer his questions about God—and you might be the answer to that prayer. Somewhere right now there is a person praying for her elderly grandparent who lives far away and is in need of conversation and friendship—and you might be the answer to that prayer.

Somewhere right now there are millions of people praying to God to meet a felt need—and you and I very well could be the answer to their prayers. God is not a genie in a bottle who snaps His fingers, making things poof into existence at our beck and call. I want to be careful here as I say this, so as not to speak heresy or sell God short, because God did in fact speak the universe into existence (Genesis 1). God did divinely provide manna every morning for the Israelites to eat (Exodus 16). There are times when God takes charge and makes things happen without us. But in my understanding of Scripture, once God spoke the universe into existence He set about natural rules, laws, and commands by which the world would function from that point forward. Embedded in that process is the need for us to engage one another in relationship and to bring about His good works in others' lives.

Can God simply speak things into existence or speak things into exile in our lives? Yes. But it's foolish to think that God will answer every prayer that way. God has created us and expects us to do the good works He has prepared in advance for us to do (Ephesians 2:10). And those good works He has prepared in advance for us to do are the answers to other people's prayers. After experiencing my own missed opportunities and hearing about the heartbreaking nature of others', I came across this quote from Winston Churchill that hit a little too close to home:

> To each there comes in their lifetime a special moment when they are figuratively tapped on the shoulder and offered the chance to do a very special thing, unique to them and fitted to their talents. What a tragedy if that moment finds them unprepared or unqualified for that which could have been their finest hour.

As I look back on my life, I would certainly consider my divine appointment conversations to be some of the finest hours of my life. Those divine moments were times when I knew I was where I needed to be, doing what needed to be done, and living in the Spirit. *There are no finer hours or more meaningful moments in this life than when we are connecting people to God. What a tragedy to go through life unprepared and unresponsive to the divine opportunities God prepared in advance for us.*

Mark Batterson wrote a best-selling book, *Circle Maker: Praying Circles Around Your Biggest Dreams and Greatest Fears.* Think about the hundreds of thousands of prayers that book has set off in people's hearts. Do you think that God is going to answer all those prayers with a snap of His fingers and no help from His fellow workers? Or do you think God will prompt people in their social circles into action so that they will partner with them to see those prayers come to fruition? I want to be careful not to create a false dichotomy here; this is not an either/or but rather a both/and. God does both. God speaks into existence answers to some prayers, AND He sends out His fellow workers (you and me) to bring answers to other prayers. As we seek God in our quiet time, listen to His voice, and follow the promptings of the Holy Spirit, we may be the answer to the prayers that were set off in the hearts of readers of the *Circle Maker* book . . . and the prayers of many others. But it is heartbreaking to know that many of those prayers set off by Batterson's book may go unanswered because of our disobedience in following through on God's promptings.

Philip, God's Co-Worker

Here's one more biblical example to drive this home—there are many more throughout Scripture. This example of Philip, a disciple of Christ, is one chapter ahead of Paul's conversion in the book of Acts, chapter 8:26–40. Here Philip is prompted into action to answer the call of God to tend to an Ethiopian who is reading Scripture and in need of direction.

> Now an angel of the Lord said to Philip, "Go south to the road—the desert road—that goes down from Jerusalem to Gaza." So he started out, and on his way he met an Ethiopian eunuch, an important official in charge of all the treasury of the Kandake (which means "queen of the Ethiopians"). This man had gone to Jerusalem to worship, and on his way home was sitting in his chariot reading the Book of Isaiah the prophet. The Spirit told Philip, "Go to that chariot and stay near it."

Then Philip ran up to the chariot and heard the man reading Isaiah the prophet. "Do you understand what you are reading?" Philip asked.

"How can I," he said, "unless someone explains it to me?" So he invited Philip to come up and sit with him.

This is the passage of Scripture the eunuch was reading:

"He was led like a sheep to the slaughter,
    and as a lamb before its shearer is silent,
        so he did not open his mouth.
In his humiliation he was deprived of justice.
    Who can speak of his descendants?
        For his life was taken from the earth."

The eunuch asked Philip, "Tell me, please, who is the prophet talking about, himself or someone else?" Then Philip began with that very passage of Scripture and told him the good news about Jesus.

As they traveled along the road, they came to some water and the eunuch said, "Look, here is water. What can stand in the way of my being baptized?" And he gave orders to stop the chariot. Then both Philip and the eunuch went down into the water and Philip baptized him. When they came up out of the water, the Spirit of the Lord suddenly took Philip away, and the eunuch did not see him again, but went on his way rejoicing. Philip, however, appeared at Azotus and traveled about, preaching the gospel in all the towns until he reached Caesarea.

God could have reached this Ethiopian in a thousand different ways. He could have convicted his heart by sending the Holy Spirit upon him. The Ethiopian could have fallen asleep, and God could have revealed Jesus to him in a dream. God could have sent an angel to reveal the answer to the prophecy of Isaiah. However, God chose to send Philip as the answer to prayer for this Ethiopian.

Who's at the table next to you at the coffee shop who might be sitting in confusion over God's great mysteries? Who's in the Uber pool ride with you who might be toiling over the meaning of life? Who's sitting with you at your kids' tee-ball end-of-season party who might be lost and looking for a church, just waiting for an invitation?

You might be thinking, "Wow, that last tee-ball party illustration was awfully specific." Well, there's a reason for that. This was a divine opportunity my wife and I found ourselves in a little over a year ago.

Our kids David and Makenna had just finished their first season of tee-ball. And we were looking for a table to sit at for the banquet. There was another couple sitting at a table with their two girls, who were on our team. The tee-ball league was our first meeting with this couple, and, to be honest, we didn't really get to know them very well during the short season. Anyone with little kids knows that it's challenging to get much conversation in amongst all the commotion and chaos of kids running around with bats in hand and wild throws swirling about. It's everything you can do just to get through three innings of this madness.

So we sat down with this couple, reintroduced ourselves, and began chatting with Gabriel and Leilani. As Gabriel began asking us about ourselves and what we were up to, we began to talk about our church, community, and how much we were loving where we were at. Gabriel then mentioned that they had just been talking about needing to find a church. However, neither of them had much knowledge of church or places to even start looking. As it turned out, Leilani had moved to a universalist approach to faith—the notion that there is a god and that perhaps god is really just the universe. That was going to be the type of church they started searching for first.

As we talked, my wife and I invited them to check out our church, and we exchanged numbers. A couple of weeks went by, and we followed up with them. We re-extended the invitation a couple of times, and Gabriel and Leilani showed up to church with their two girls a few weeks later. The first time they attended church, Gabriel accepted Christ at the end of the service. A few weeks later, Leilani accepted Christ as her Lord and Savior. And a few weeks after that, they got baptized together in front of the church and their two precious daughters.

My wife and I just recently were catching up with them, and we asked them how things were going one year later. Gabriel and Leilani shared with us that Christ had changed nearly every aspect of their lives. Their marriage had done a 180, and they were engaging as a couple in a better way than they ever had before. Their parenting had changed, and they were leading their girls in a way they never had before. After signing up to serve on the tech team at church, Gabriel discovered a new passion for videography that he had never experienced before.

It's phenomenal to see how much this couple has changed as a result of Christ entering their lives, and it's wonderful to see how much our church has been impacted by their entering our community. All that because they had been thinking and praying about checking out a church, and it turned out my wife and I had been the answer to their prayer.

I realize that divine opportunities can be a bit risky, complex, and challenging at times. However, what I have learned from my study of missed opportunities sits in line with this quote from Dennis Waitley: "While life is inherently risky. There is only one big risk you should avoid at all costs, and that is the risk of doing nothing." I would rather go out on a limb and risk looking foolish for a moment in conversation than walk away having missed yet another opportunity—knowing that my disobedience is not a neutral act. My disobedience impacts the lives of others. And it's incredibly selfish and cruel for me to miss an opportunity for someone to be touched by God because I didn't want to risk experiencing mild social discomfort.

I think this is one of the missing ingredients to restoring the faith in America and around the world. Think about if each Christian in your city had one divine appointment each week with someone in their neighborhood, workplace, or shopping centers. Now that could spark a movement throughout your city on an unprecedented scale. And just think of the prayers that could be answered and the belief in God that could be confirmed.

> Never treat a divine assignment lightly. God has legions of angels anxious to do His bidding yet He asks YOU to do it! (Richard Blackaby)

DISCUSSION QUESTIONS

1. What does it mean to you when you read that "we are God's fellow workers"? What does that look like in your life, right now?

2. Do you agree or disagree with the statement that our disobedience is not a neutral act, that other people's lives are negatively impacted by our disobedience? What is one scenario in which someone's disobedience to a divine opportunity could negatively impact someone else's life?

3. Identify one person in your life for whom you could be the answer to their prayer for hope, support, friendship, financial provision, job referral, etc.? What one step could you take this week to reach out and check in?

Moving from Missed Opportunity to Heart Transformation

God knows the eternal consequences of
every action, of every act of obedience or
disobedience to His word.
—Blackaby Ministries

The Blackabys point out the simple fact that there are consequences to every act of obedience or disobedience to God's Word. Each act of obedience or disobedience has implications for our intimacy and connection with God, as well as for our intimacy and connection with the people around us. The truth is that while God knows the eternal consequences of *every* action, we have no way of knowing the eternal consequences of *any* action. One of life's great mysteries is that our action and inaction are weighted in ways we do not know. This is why we must be obedient and trusting of God's Word and the promptings that He puts on our hearts. *When it comes to divine promptings, wouldn't you much rather be obedient and wrong than be disobedient and right?*

Let me give you a quick example. I once heard the pastor, author, and speaker Francis Chan share about a time when he was preparing at a nearby coffee shop for a Sunday morning message. As he was packing up to leave, he noticed a gentleman sitting off to the side reading. Francis felt as though God were prompting him to go over, say hello, and introduce himself. But that was it. Francis didn't receive any further prompting for the conversation. He thought to himself, "That would be kind of a weird thing to do without anything else to say." So Francis finished packing up to leave, ignored the prompting, and headed off toward the church.

Francis couldn't get this prompting out of his head, though, and began to feel strongly convicted of his disobedience. After getting halfway to the church, Francis turned around and went back to the coffee shop. He looked in through the window and saw the guy still sitting there reading. So Francis went back inside, walked up to the guy, and said, "Hi, sorry to interrupt. I just wanted to introduce myself. I'm Francis. You might think this is kind of weird, but I just felt like God wanted me to come over here and introduce myself and say hi to you." The guy said, "I don't think that's weird." Francis replied, "Well, that's it. Just wanted to say hi. Have a great day." Then Francis headed back out the door. No wowing moment, no glorious ending. Just a divine hello and an introduction and he was back on the road.

You might be thinking, "Even though that guy didn't think it was weird, I do." But here's the point: we are only seeing one small snapshot of this gentleman's life. What if at lunch God prompts another Christian to go up to him and introduce himself and say hi from God? What if at dinner God prompts another Christian to go up to him and introduce himself and say hi from God? After two or three of these interactions, now he will find it weird, to the point that God will have his full attention. However, if only two of the three people are obedient, the sequence of actions loses its full effect. If only one person is obedient it loses even more affect.

Do you see the point? We have no possible way of knowing the eternal consequences of our obedience or disobedience. What seems odd, weird, or even misguided could be the key moment amongst a series of interactions this person has had before us or after us that unlock a divine revelation for them. What a shame it would be to find out that you were the only one who was disobedient and that you were the missing link to an otherwise powerful moment in the spiritual life of another person.

One of the craziest and most unpredictable moments, in this regard, was relayed to me by a friend, Jennifer, whose mom responded with obedience to the most odd prompting you've probably ever heard. This friend shared the following divine appointment about her mother, Linda:

We were at a nice big church that was filled with a lot of well-to-do people. My dad was the guest speaker that day. In the middle of the worship set, God spoke to my mom and told her to go pray for a woman who was sitting near the front. The woman had expensive jewelry and clothes on and looked unapproachable.

God told my mom to go pray for her and place her pinky on the woman's forehead. My mom stood there wrestling with this, arguing with God, and begging him, "Please, not here—not that woman. I'm going to embarrass myself and my husband. We don't even go here; we are guests!" She even asked God if she could do it after the service. He said, "Do it now."

Fortunately, my mom had experienced enough divine appointments in her life to be obedient to even this weird, seemingly random prompting. She gave in and made her brave walk around the aisles and over to the woman. Without saying a word, she walked up and placed her pinky on the woman's forehead. The woman broke down, sobbing.

My mom asked, "What? Why did God tell me to do that?" She told my mom that she had received a diagnosis of severe cancer and that she felt hopeless and wondered whether God cared or was even real. She had asked God, "If you are real and do care, send someone over to pray for me. But, so I know it's really you, have them place their pinky on my forehead." My mom was able to pray and minister to her that day.

Doesn't that divine appointment sound insane! It's one of the best reminders of the craziness of God that we have no idea what others might just have prayed and what God might be up to. The only way to find out is to be obedient—even to those craziest of promptings. If we are disobedient we will never find out whether this was a genuine prompting from God, and we also risk leaving someone else's prayer unanswered.

We Live What We Believe

Another way the Blackabys have positioned disobedience is by saying:

If you have an obedience problem, you have a love problem. . . . There are two words in the Christian's language that cannot go together: "No, Lord." If you say "no," He is not your Lord. If He is your Lord, your answer must always be "yes." . . . When God invites you to join Him and you face a crisis of belief, what you do next reveals what you believe about God. . . . What you do—not what you *say* you believe—reveals what you really believe about God.

Dallas Willard put it this way, "People live what they truly believe. The genuine beliefs of a person are made obvious by what they do."

That's some hard-hitting stuff right there. I remember the first time I read that Dallas Willard quote it was like a bucket of cold water being thrown in my face. Both of those are quotes to sit and ponder for a moment. Consider just a few questions in this regard: How often do you read the Bible? How often do you spend time in prayerful communion with God? How often are you giving others an opportunity to experience God? What would your answers indicate about the reality of your belief in God?

For example, a student of mine, Ali, told me about a time when her non-Christian friend asked her whether she had read the entire Bible. Ali, in all honesty, had to reply, "I've read a good portion of it, but not all of it." The non-Christian friend said, "I'm realizing how many Christians have never even read the entire Bible. I just assumed that if you had dedicated your life to it that you would have read it." That was a wake-up call and a turning point in Ali's life where she began to take Bible reading seriously.

If you truly believed that the Bible is indeed the inspired Word of God, how would you not find time to read it every day? If you truly believed that prayer is indeed time spent communing with God, how would you not find time to pray and wait patiently for a response from God? If you truly believed that through Christ we bring Good News that has POWER—His life-raising, sick-healing, hell-crushing POWER—how would you not find someone to encourage in Christ every day?

Understand, therefore, that the Lord your God is indeed God. (Deuteronomy 7:9 NLT)

Let's state it this way: if you truly believed that the Bible is indeed the inspired Word of God, why would you spend three hours a day viewing social media, Netflix, YouTube, and TV and zero time in the Word? If you truly believed that prayer is indeed time spent communing with God, why would you spend thirty minutes checking and rechecking your phone for replies to text messages and social media posts without being able to sit still for more than two minutes before giving up on hearing back from God? If you truly believed that through Christ we bring Good News of a life-raising, sick-healing, hell-crushing power, why would you walk around barricading yourself from people with your sunglasses, phone, and earbuds?

You live what you truly believe. Your genuine beliefs are made obvious by what you do. Being brutally honest with your self-assessment of your faith is crucial. This should be a regular practice for every Christian. For example, Christians who regularly walk around with earbuds in their ears are a dead giveaway that they are still living for themselves and not for God. You cannot say you believe in the two greatest commandments—love the Lord your God with all your heart, soul, and mind, and love your neighbor as yourself—and the Great Commission—go and give others an opportunity to experience God—and then walk around everywhere with earbuds in your ears. This is why the brutally honest self-evaluation is so essential. As we say in our house: You better check yourself before you wreck yourself!

Check Yourself Before You Wreck Yourself

My friend Julian Lowe once said, "God allows injuries to save us from wounds. God allows wounds to save us from death. God allows death to save us from destruction." From Julian's perspective, God allows injuries because we are on our way to being wounded. God allows wounds because we are on our way to death. Perhaps God allows missed opportunity injuries because without that recognition, without that awakening experience, we would be on our way to missing yet another opportunity that is even larger and more significant in terms of eternal consequences.

At what point will you repent and turn to God? Will it be after missed opportunity injuries? Missed opportunity wounds? Missed opportunity deaths? God gives you gradual warnings about your disobedience and missed opportunities. He is a gracious and merciful God who is patiently waiting for you to repent and turn to Him. He is patiently waiting for you to check yourself before you wreck yourself.

This section of chapters will help you do just that. In the chapters "Good Grief," "God's Grace," and "Go Forth" I will walk you through the process of moving from missed opportunity to heart transformation. After interviewing over fifty people about divine appointments and missed opportunities, I have identified a pattern of recovery from missed opportunities. This recovery process works for those who have experienced missed opportunity injuries, wounds, and even death.

Some of the most heart-wrenching stories were those I heard people share when they knew they had missed a clear opportunity for conversation with someone and within a short time found out that the person had committed suicide, passed away from illness, or died in a car accident. While these people experienced conviction of some of the most tragic missed opportunities, they ended up with the most dynamic obedience after going through the healing process with the full immersion of God's discipline, grace, and redemption. The people who experienced the most tragic missed opportunities later ended up with the most dynamic of divine appointments by using the missed opportunity as motivation in the future. Let this be your opportunity to fully experience God's good grief, God's grace, and a renewed motivation to go forth into the opportunities of the future.

Disclaimer

I need to frame the chapters in this section a bit before you begin reading them. These chapters are NOT meant for just anybody that's ever had anything tragic happen to a loved one. It's more particular than that. These chapters are specifically for people that have received a prompting/ nudging from God, in some way, to say something or do something and they ignored it or let it go. I just want to be clear that the language in these chapters of "missed opportunity" or "disobedience" are NOT meant for just any type of situation. It's not disobedience if you never received a prompting to begin with. These are chapters specific to times where people actually felt prompted by God to do something or say something and they ignored it.

DISCUSSION QUESTIONS

1. How often do you read the Bible? How often do you spend time in prayerful communion with God? How often are you giving others an opportunity to experience God? What would your answers indicate about the reality of your belief in God?

2. Do you agree or disagree with the quote from the Blackabys: "There are two words in the Christian's language that cannot go together: 'No, Lord.' If you say 'no,' He is not your Lord. If He is your Lord, your answer must always be 'yes'"? In what practical way could this play out in your daily walk with God?

3. Do you agree or disagree with the quote from Dallas Willard: "People live what they truly believe. The genuine beliefs of a person are made obvious by what they do"? Think of one example in which you could point to someone's behavior being the genuine belief that is in contrast to what they might say they believe?

Godly Grief

Failure is only the opportunity to begin again,
this time more wisely.
—Anonymous

I believe it's beneficial in the long run for everyone, at some point in their life, to come face-to-face with the consequences of a missed opportunity. Hopefully, not one where someone loses their life or is physically harmed, but one in which the consequences can be seen, felt, identified, and owned. There are elements of spiritual growth and life-giving motivation that can be achieved only through the grieving and healing process of a missed moment with God. Important to note is that *while there may be missed opportunities, there are no wasted opportunities.* When we allow God to take us through the healing process from missed moments, we are presented with the opportunity to begin again, this time more wisely and with more motivation.

Jeremy, a pastor in Missouri, shared the following missed opportunity story with me from when he was a college student and volunteer youth leader. Jeremy's experience will be revisited in the following two chapters ("God's Grace" and "Go Forth"), as it highlights the full healing process necessary to bounce back from even the most tragic of missed opportunities.

> I was a volunteer youth leader when I was in college. I volunteered under the same youth pastor for about five years. We were at two different churches during that time, and we were in the second church for the last two years that I worked with him. This church had a particularly tough group, because they had been through six youth pastors in like two years or some ridiculous amount of time. So some of the students weren't really receptive to having another new pastor. This made trying to build relationships really hard.
>
> After a while, our group had really grown from just a handful of kids to running a hundred or so on a weekly basis. I wish that they were all seeking Christ with all their heart, but that wasn't the case. However, they were bringing friends, and we were grateful for that.
>
> I remember that there were a couple of guys who were kind of trouble makers that I had to come down hard on sometimes, but I had started to get some camaraderie going with them. These two high school guys brought a friend one week. I met him, and I wish I would have taken more time to get to know him and draw him in, but you know the busyness of life sometimes—you just don't take the time. I think he may have come back once more the next week, but I still didn't get a chance to connect with him.
>
> It was about a month after I remembered meeting him that the students came into the youth ministry that night and many of them looked rather depressed. I was like, "What's going on?" and they said, "Our friend killed himself yesterday." I asked which friend, and they told me his name. I remembered only the first name of the kid I had met a month earlier and asked, "Is that the kid who was here four weeks ago?" And they were like, "Yeah."
>
> In that moment, as a college student wanting to be a youth pastor and just having this burden for souls, it hit me really hard.

Maybe even feeling overly responsible for that, like somehow it was my fault—that's kind of an exaggeration of what I felt, but there was a feeling of responsibility like, I could have made a difference. I could have said something, I could have taken the time. That kid passed through our student ministry, and he talked to me and I missed it. I felt like there should have been a sign. There were a lot of would have, should have, could haves running through my mind in that moment.

He was one of two boys in his family, and his older brother had committed suicide on the same day the year prior. He had idolized his brother, and he went down to the same place that his brother had killed himself and took his own life the same way in the same spot on the same day. Thinking back to that moment, I don't feel guilty anymore, but I do feel like, Lord, was there something I should have known, something I missed? That was the missed opportunity with all the regret and all the feelings of guilt and responsibility attached to missing something.

The question I asked myself was, Did I fail to recognize something? Was I not in tune with the Holy Spirit? I took a lot of the responsibility on myself. I couldn't blame God in that moment—like, God, you didn't sound the alarm—because I believe God is caring. I believe anybody who crossed this boy's path could have and should have made a difference in his life. And that one sticks out to me because I ask myself what I could have done, what I could have said. Could I have been a little more sensitive or inquisitive? You know, something besides "How are you?" and "What's your name?" I didn't even take the time to ask about his family or siblings. That would have been an alarm right there, had I asked about his siblings.

I just introduced myself and his friends introduced him, and we high-fived and shook hands. It was such a nondescript conversation because it was the three of them, two kids I knew and this kid. There was nothing memorable about the conversation, and there should have been.

The interaction with him is that part that affected me the most because it was so unmemorable and impersonal. You know, you greet the new kid and say hi to the students you know. I think that's why I took it so hard because as a youth worker you feel like he was in the palm of your hand and you let him slip away. And there's that feeling of responsibility and guilt—that could have, should have, would have regret. And that to me was a defining moment of my Christian walk and faith, to do everything you can to not let a person slip through your grasp. That's not necessarily realistic because of the number of students we deal with sometimes, but the hope is that I walk with a little bit more awareness or sensitivity.

God brought him to me, he came to my doorstep, and I missed it, not because I was uncaring or unloving—I was just insensitive, busy, and distracted. Honestly, I had a to-do list that needed to get done. That's not a good excuse. I don't even remember what I was supposed to be doing; we were getting ready for student service that night, and I was probably playing in the band and/or maybe speaking. But the fact that I don't remember means that, unfortunately, it probably wasn't that significant.

Sometimes we overlook relationships for the other things we have to get done or check off our box; we trade relationships for responsibility. In student ministry relationships are my responsibility, and I missed it that night. I don't know what I was supposed to be doing, but I know the encounter was "I'm going to say hi to my two guys and meet their friend so I've done my obligatory greet, and then I'll go take care of the business that really matters"—and I got it backwards. I should have taken care of business that really mattered by hanging with that kid or making sure I connected with him, like, "Hey guys, I got to take care of some stuff, but I want to connect with you before I leave today." I do that now, now that I know I've missed it. There are times when I'll be like, "Guys, I have to be on stage in like three minutes, but I'll take you guys out to McDonalds and we'll get a coke after this. Cool, alright?" I learned it that day the hard way.

Maybe I'm taking on too much of the blame for every Christian who passes through my life, but I do feel like I had the chance to be a difference maker in his life and missed it. It's like when you're playing a close basketball game and there's ten seconds left and your team's down by two points and you get to take the final shot and miss, and your team loses the big game. Well, there are a bunch of people who missed shots previously in the game, but you took the last shot at the last second and missed. You feel the weight of it, like it's your fault the team lost. There were likely people who missed far easier shots, lay-ups, or free throws earlier in the game, but it's the timing of the shot you missed that carries so much more weight.

Many of the feelings Jeremy highlights from this heart-wrenching story are common amongst others who have missed opportunities, both big and small. The most common words used to describe the feelings following missed opportunities are *regret*, *conviction*, and *guilt*. You're likely to be able to relate to those feelings and Jeremy's experience because of your own past missed opportunities.

Prosocial Emotion

Your feelings of regret, conviction, and guilt are natural, considering that social scientists, through the study of emotions, have discovered that we are hardwired to experience feelings of regret. In fact, regret is labeled as a prosocial emotion. It's a prosocial emotion because feelings of regret actually keep us from continually doing harm to others. The feelings of regret, remorse, conviction, guilt, and grief that arise after we hurt someone emotionally, physically, or spiritually cause us to stop and experience a teachable moment. Without those prosocial emotions we'd have little awareness of the harm we've done and little motivation to keep us from continuing to cause such harm.

This is one of the reasons I would say that it's better to experience a tragic missed opportunity than to go through life thinking you haven't missed any opportunities at all. In my research, it was the people with the most tragic missed opportunities who became the most teachable, motivated, and passionate about making the most of every opportunity thereafter. The factor that made some scenarios more tragic than others was seeing the heart-wrenching end result of the missed opportunity. When we are confronted with the consequence of our missed opportunity, it takes on eternal meaning and significance that cannot be ignored. It forces us to take an inventory on our life priorities and re-evaluate our awareness of and obedience to God's promptings.

Unfortunately, when people go through life completely unaware of the consequences of their missed opportunities, they never receive the blessing of God's good grief. If you never get a chance to see the consequences that unfold as a result of your disobedience and inaction, there is no motivation to change your ways. I believe that it's healthy to reach a place in life where you have a rude awakening, see and feel the consequences of your inaction, and become disgusted by your own disobedience. That disgust over disobedience leads you to reflect, analyze, and re-evaluate your faith in a way that leads to correction and godly guidance for the future.

In 2 Corinthians 7:8–11 the apostle Paul is writing to the church of Corinth as a follow-up to a letter he had written them previously. In the previous letter, Paul had to address disobedience and unrighteous behavior in the church. Below, Paul is reflecting upon the good that came from the grief, conviction, and guilt his previous letter had brought upon them. Paul points out the spiritual growth that occurred because of God's good grief:

> For even if I made you grieve with my letter, I do not regret it—though I did regret it, for I see that that letter grieved you, though only for a while. As it is, I rejoice, not because you were grieved, but because you were grieved into repenting. For you felt a godly grief, so that you suffered no loss through us.
>
> For godly grief produces a repentance that leads to salvation without regret, whereas

worldly grief produces death. For see what earnestness this godly grief has produced in you, but also what eagerness to clear yourselves, what indignation, what fear, what longing, what zeal, what punishment! At every point you have proved yourselves innocent in the matter. (ESV)

As the apostle Paul points out, godly grief causes us to repent and turn to God, to repent of disobedience and turn to obedience, to repent of inaction and be stirred to action. Every Christian needs to seriously contemplate their missed opportunities, explore the possible eternal consequences, and turn to God. If you do, you have God's promise that the experience will lead you to salvation without regret and produce in you a sense of readiness, eagerness, and zeal for the opportunities to come.

Friends, Don't Let Friends Avoid Grief

I'll never forget an exchange between two students over this issue of missed opportunities and feelings of regret. While we were discussing and sharing experiences with divine appointments and missed opportunities, a student spoke up to share a missed opportunity of her own.

Over the summer, I went to the east coast to serve at a Christian youth camp. At the end of the camp, I packed up and was heading back to California. After I went through the lines of security and bag-check at the airport, I finally settled into a seat in the terminal as I waited for my flight. While sitting there, I noticed this older man across the terminal who was sitting slouched over and looking very sad. As I was looking at him, I felt this urge to go over and talk with him, see how he was doing, and simply pray for him. But I couldn't help but think how awkward this would be for a college student to approach an older man and pray for him. So I didn't.

As we began to line up to board the flight, he ended up in the line with me for the same flight. Again, I felt this prompting to talk with him and pray for him. But I just couldn't bring myself to do it. Then after we all boarded the flight, he was sitting just a few seats away from me. He still looked sad and distraught, and I still felt the prompting to pray for him. But I just couldn't do it, and the longer I waited the more public and challenging the situation became.

Finally the flight landed and we all unloaded, grabbed our luggage, and went our separate ways. With each passing opportunity, I felt more regret. I know it was a missed opportunity, and I wish I could go back to that moment in the terminal and have a redo. I would have taken advantage of that very first opportunity that presented itself. I would have approached him, talked with him, and prayed for him.

As we continued to discuss her missed opportunity as a class, another student chimed in and said:

You know what, I wouldn't feel bad about it. You don't know that it was necessarily a missed opportunity. In fact, it might be better that you didn't approach him. It could have been unsafe for a young woman to approach an older man like that. You never know what his deal was and what he was capable of. You could have been putting yourself in danger by approaching him.

I'll be honest—up until she said that I hadn't at all considered this girl's safety. The way she described the situation didn't sound as though there were a safety concern. Plus, I tend to assume that if God is presenting us with opportunities, nudgings, and promptings, He will provide the protection to go with it. But I stopped and thought for a moment, "Maybe she's right; maybe there could have been safety concerns." Then it hit me: "Wait a second, this girl was sitting in an airport terminal; there's literally no safer place she could have been to have a divine conversation with this man. All these people had been through metal detectors, bags had been scanned, video cameras were in every corner of the room, people were all around, and security guards and police officers were present. There's probably no safer place in the world she could have been for this divine opportunity."

(Please note, I'm not saying that there aren't unsafe conditions that shouldn't be rethought, but this just doesn't sound like one of them. Know that I'm not advocating for chasing people down dark alleyways late at night to try to pray for them, but let's also be careful not to create unnecessary safety bubbles before we are willing to connect and care for people in conversation. Simply use godly discernment and common sense.)

It was in that interaction between two female students that I realized the damage that can come when we rob each other of experiencing the blessing of godly grief. *It's vital for spiritual growth that friends don't let friends avoid godly grief.* When we let people off the hook for missed opportunities, we deny them the experience of godly grief that leads to repentance; salvation without regret; and a sense of readiness, eagerness, and zeal for the opportunities to come. When we let ourselves and others off the hook for missed opportunities, we deny and delay the transformational learning experience that could have come from necessary spiritual pains of regret.

The devil also wants in on this action. I believe there is spiritual warfare that goes into this as well. When we miss opportunities, without ever seeing or hearing the consequences of our disobedience and inaction, we enter dangerous territory of self-justification and rationalization. Generally speaking, after we miss an opportunity we tend to rationalize away our regret. The devil gets into our head and causes us to think:

"No, you didn't miss anything there. That wasn't a divine opportunity. That wasn't a prompting from God. That wasn't a spiritual prompting—that was just you, that was all in your head. It's better that you let that moment pass. The conversation would have been awkward; that person could have been offended or weirded out. You missed nothing—no need to worry or over-think it. I'm sure they're doing just fine; they were probably just tired, not sad. Just enjoy your time on your phone; you might be missing out on a connection through social media. You need this moment for your own emotional health. You do you, and don't worry about them. You need those earbuds in to listen to your music to get you in the right mindset for your long day ahead. You didn't have time for that conversation anyway. You've got other responsibilities to get to, so don't get distracted by these people around you. That would have been a distraction, not an opportunity."

What the devil, and well-intentioned friends, do in that moment is allow you to justify and rationalize away the missed opportunity. As a result, you justify and rationalize away the godly grief, the teachable moment, and the need to repent that would have transformed your heart into one of obedience in the future.

> Blessed is the one you discipline, LORD,
>   the one you teach from your law;
> you grant them relief from days of trouble . . .
> (Psalm 94:12–13)

The Absence of Pain

In a message by Ravi Zacharias about necessary and unnecessary pain and suffering, he talked about a young girl named Ashlyn Blocker who had a rare disease called congenital insensitivity to pain with anhidrosis (CIPA). This condition left Ashlyn with the inability to experience any physical pain. Ashlyn's mom, Tara Blocker, said, "Some people would say that's a good thing. But no, it's not. Pain is there for a reason. It lets your body know something's wrong and needs to be fixed. I'd give anything for her to feel pain."

Children growing up with this genetic disorder experience countless health issues and serious injuries that go unnoticed because of the lack of pain that would have otherwise tipped them off to the injury. The lack of pain to bring awareness of the injury often leads to further complications. Some of these kids have walked around on a broken ankle that occurred from jumping down stairs, only to be discovered when parents notice discoloration and swelling of the ankle. At least in these cases, the outward physical symptoms of swelling and bruising tip them off to attend to the injury. But it's the infections with no outward symptoms that cause the most concern, as there is no way to detect the illness at all. There's a serious inward issue with no outward symptom to alert them to the problem.

All the issues Ashlyn Blocker has experienced because of her lack of pain led her mother, Tara, to say, "Every night my prayer is the same: 'God, please allow Ashlyn to feel pain.'" This really hit me hard. I am now at the point where my prayer is the same for the millions of Christians who continue to miss divine opportunity after divine opportunity without ever recognizing the eternal consequences of their disobedience, inaction, and avoidance of others.

"God, please allow us to feel the pain of our missed opportunities so that we may be made aware of the outward consequences that are resulting from our inward heart problems. Allow us to see and feel the outward pain of the consequences of our inaction so that we can be alert to the need of inner transformation of our heart. Allow us to experience godly grief so that we can repent and turn to You. God, please use Your godly grief to produce in us a readiness, eagerness, and zeal for the opportunities to come. May You give us eyes to see the unseen, ears to hear the unheard, and a heart for people so that we see them as an opportunity and not an obstruction. In Jesus' name, Amen."

Friends Don't Let Friends Turn Godly Grief into Shameful Bondage

Failure is an event, not a person. (Zig Ziglar)

While friends shouldn't allow you to avoid the godly grief necessary for life transformation, they on the other hand shouldn't allow to you linger so long in the grief, regret, conviction, and guilt that it turns into shameful bondage. This is where the other aspect of spiritual warfare can come into play. The devil is up to a couple of different tricks here. One, as mentioned above, is that he wants you to remain blind to the consequences of your disobedience and inaction and miss the spiritual growth process that occurs through godly grief. However, should you become aware of a tragic consequence that resulted from a missed opportunity and feel regret, conviction, and guilt, he wants to turn that grief into shame. This is why the apostle Paul pointed out that "godly grief produces a repentance that leads to salvation without regret, whereas worldly grief produces death" (2 Corinthians 7:10 ESV). We must be careful to work through godly grief with care and intentionality.

We have to be careful that we experience godly grief (conviction) and not worldly grief (condemnation). Godly grief is the conviction of the Holy Spirit; it's necessary, correcting, and healthy. Worldly grief is the condemnation the evil one uses to bring shame, disgrace, and bondage. The Bible teaches us that the devil seeks to turn your grief from godly to worldly so that it produces spiritual death. The worldly grief will paralyze you and disqualify you. Worldly grief tends to turn into shame and bondage; it keeps you from future obedience and leads you to disqualify yourself from being worthy of being used by God.

John 10:10 tells us that the devil came to steal, kill, and destroy. This includes your sense of self-worth, value, and dignity. And there's no better way to do that than to use your missed opportunities—especially those after which you discovered a tragic consequence to your disobedience. John 8:44 tells us that the devil is the author of lies. The devil is incapable of telling the truth. He either straight up tells boldfaced lies or he manipulates the truth into a lie. You will be able to recognize the voice of the devil, most commonly in this regard, through your own inner critic and negative self-talk. Therefore, you must keep close watch over your inner voice to make sure your thoughts and feelings are those of godly grief, not worldly grief.

My friend Julian Lowe once pointed out to me the good news that comes from this bad news of spiritual warfare. He said, "The good news is that since the devil tells nothing but lies, when he does tell us those lies, he actually tips us off to the truth." When you begin to clarify and label the source of your thoughts, you will quickly begin to identify those that are from God and those that are from the devil. God plants seeds for sustainable self-growth, while the devil plants seeds for mutilated self-discipline. God uses discipline that equips and empowers, while the devil uses discipline that demoralizes and defeats.

God wants you to be motivated by the freedom of salvation, while the devil wants you to be held in the bondage of condemnation.

In this process of godly grief, you must learn to recognize the voice of God and reject the voice of the devil. Jesus in John 10:2–5 unpacks this for us:

> The one who enters by the gate is the shepherd of the sheep. . . . The sheep listen to his voice. He calls his own sheep by name and leads them out. . . . His sheep follow him because they know his voice. But they will never follow a stranger; in fact, they will run away from him because they do not recognize a stranger's voice.

This is why it is so important to regularly be in the Word. You need to intimately study and learn to discern the genuine, authentic voice of God. Then you will be able to quickly identify the counterfeit voice of the devil. First John 4:1 states, "Dear friends, do not believe every spirit, but test the spirits to see whether they are from God, because many false prophets have gone out into the world." I would add to that last clause—and into your head.

In order to stay on track with godly grief without slipping over into worldly grief, you must constantly improve your speed and accuracy in terms of your recognition of and obedience to God's voice, as well as of your recognition and rejection of the devil's voice. We've all been taught to pray and ask for things in Jesus' name, but we also need to learn to rebuke things in Jesus' name. When negative self-talk pops into your head, you must quickly identify it as a lie from the devil, rebuke the thought in the name of Jesus, and replace it with the truth of Scripture.

Be mindful that the devil is trying to manipulate your self-improvement process with mutilated self-discipline that leads to worldly grief. We need to spot and squash it immediately with God's Word and quickly get back on track with godly grief. Let me give you some examples. If you hear the thought in your head, "I'm worthless—I always make the same old mistakes," you have to immediately identify that as a lie, remember that the devil has now tipped you off to the truth, and replace it with God's truth: "I can do all things through [Christ,] who gives me strength" (Philippians 4:13)." If you hear the lie "I'm a loser. I know better than this, and I can't ever get it right," immediately swap out that lie for the truth "The Lord is my helper; I will not be afraid" (Hebrews 13:6). If you hear the lie "I'm worthless to God. I will never be spiritually mature enough to be used for a divine appointment," immediately squash that lie and replace it with the truth that God "is able to do immeasurably more than all we ask or imagine" (Ephesians 3:20).

When you self-criticize, it's because you're not satisfied with your performance or obedience to God and have a desire to be and do better. God appreciates the underlying sentiment to be and do better, but He has another path for leading you to that place of self-improvement, spiritual growth, and spiritual maturity. And it comes through the transformative power of the Holy Spirit.

Rearview Christianity

I believe that this quote from Alexander Graham Bell puts proper godly grief into perspective: "Don't look so long and regretfully upon the closed door that we do not see the one that has opened for us." Todd White has used the description "Rearview Christianity" to describe the result of worldly grief. Worldly grief gets us stuck, paralyzed, bound up in shame, and looking in the rearview mirror, focused intently on the mistakes of our past. Godly grief gets us unstuck and motivates us through spiritual maturity as we become eager for the opportunities to come. *You don't want to look so long and regretfully upon the missed opportunities of the past that you don't see the divine opportunities of the present.*

Finally, godly grief tells us that we can "rejoice in our sufferings, knowing that suffering produces endurance, and endurance produces character, and character produces hope, and hope does not put us to shame, because God's love has been poured into our hearts through the Holy Spirit who has been given to us" (Romans 5:3–5 ESV). Please do not take on shame from your missed opportunities, and do not allow your friends to take on shame from their missed opportunities. Instead, grow in spiritual maturity through godly grief that produces endurance, character, and hope. I'm excited to share more of these steps toward spiritual maturity in the following chapter titled "God's Grace," which will take you through the forgiveness of God and walking in freedom.

DISCUSSION QUESTIONS

1. Think back to one time when you experienced godly grief, discipline, or conviction over something in your life. What was that experience like? What did it ultimately lead to in terms of mental, emotional, spiritual, behavioral, or lifestyle changes?

2. What is one time when you experienced worldly condemnation over something in your life? What was that experience like? How did you get out of condemnation?

3. What is one lie about yourself that keeps circulating in your mind? What is one biblical truth you could use to squash, delete, and replace that lie?

God's Grace

If you repent, I will restore you
that you may serve me;
if you utter worthy, not worthless, words,
you will be my spokesman.
—Jeremiah 15:19

The transition from godly grief to God's grace requires only one thing—repentance. There may be no stronger and more prevalent theme in the Bible than the call to repent of our sins and turn to God. This is the message that runs from the beginning of the Old Testament through the end of the New Testament. It is the message of Moses, Elijah, Elisha, Isaiah, John the Baptist, Jesus, and the apostles. It is the first message that Jesus ever preached: "Repent, for the kingdom of heaven has come near" (Matthew 4:17). It is part of the Lord's Prayer: "Forgive us our debts, as we also have forgiven our debtors" (Matthew 6:12). We are most certainly called to repent of our sins—sins of action and of inaction. Missed opportunities are sins of inaction in need of repentance and grace. "If anyone, then, knows the good they ought to do and doesn't do it, it is sin for them" (James 4:17). When we do repent, we give ourselves the opportunity to experience God's grace. For God has promised, "If you repent, I will restore . . . " (Jeremiah 15:19). Jesus' life, death, and resurrection have made it that easy.

Disqualified? Not a Chance!

If, for whatever reason, you don't feel worthy of such grace or are reluctant to receive God's forgiveness let me remind you of the story of Manasseh, the king of Judah from 2 Chronicles 33:1–17. If you ever feel as though the damage you've done is too great, please read about Manasseh and reconsider with this as a frame of reference:

> Manasseh was twelve years old when he became king, and he reigned in Jerusalem fifty-five years. He did evil in the eyes of the LORD, following the detestable practices of the nations the LORD had driven out before the Israelites. He rebuilt the high places his father Hezekiah had demolished; he also erected altars to the Baals and made Asherah poles. He bowed down to all the starry hosts and worshiped them. He built altars in the temple of the LORD, of which the LORD had said, "My Name will remain in Jerusalem forever." In both courts of the temple of the LORD, he built altars to all the starry hosts. He sacrificed his children in the fire in the Valley of Ben Hinnom, practiced divination and witchcraft, sought omens, and consulted mediums and psychics. He did much evil in the eyes of the LORD, arousing his anger.
>
> He took the image he had made and put it in God's temple, of which God had said to David and to his son Solomon, "In this temple and in Jerusalem, which I have chosen out of all the tribes of Israel, I will put my Name forever. I will not again make the feet of the Israelites leave the land I assigned to your ancestors, if only they will

be careful to do everything I commanded them concerning all the laws, decrees and regulations given through Moses." But Manasseh led Judah and the people of Jerusalem astray, so that they did more evil than the nations the LORD had destroyed before the Israelites.

The LORD spoke to Manasseh and his people, but they paid no attention. So the LORD brought against them the army commanders of the king of Assyria, who took Manasseh prisoner, put a hook in his nose, bound him with bronze shackles and took him to Babylon. In his distress he sought the favor of the LORD his God and humbled himself greatly before the God of his ancestors. And when he prayed to him, the LORD was moved by his entreaty and listened to his plea; so he brought him back to Jerusalem and to his kingdom. Then Manasseh knew that the LORD is God.

Afterward he rebuilt the outer wall of the City of David, west of the Gihon spring in the valley, as far as the entrance of the Fish Gate and encircling the hill of Ophel; he also made it much higher. He stationed military commanders in all the fortified cities in Judah.

He got rid of the foreign gods and removed the image from the temple of the LORD, as well as all the altars he had built on the temple hill and in Jerusalem; and he threw them out of the city. Then he restored the altar of the LORD and sacrificed fellowship offerings and thank offerings on it, and told Judah to serve the LORD, the God of Israel. The people, however, continued to sacrifice at the high places, but only to the LORD their God.

I'm going to go out on the limb and say that you have not led yourself or other people to do more evil than the pagan nations that the Lord had destroyed when the people of Israel entered the land. If, after all that Manasseh did, God still listened to him and was moved by his request to restore him, it's safe to assume that God will most certainly listen to your repentant request and restore you. There is nothing you could do that is beyond the reach of God's grace and forgiveness. There is no point you can reach in this life at which you are beyond restoration. There is no missed opportunity that is too tragic for God to forgive.

You will never reach a point in life where you are beyond one heartfelt prayer of repentance from God's grace, forgiveness, and restoration. So has your worst missed opportunity, one that may have resulted even in the loss of life, disqualified you from the grace of God? Not a chance. Has your most egregious oversight and avoidance of the people around you disqualified you from the work of the Lord? Not a chance. Has your greatest sin of inaction and omission disqualified you from taking part in the Great Commission? Not a chance. As my friend Julian Lowe, put it: "If God would allow Saul, a murdering persecutor of the first-century Christians, to go on to write over one-third of the New Testament; then what might God allow you to do?" The opportunities and possibilities are endless for those who repent of their sins and turn to God.

> If we confess our sins, he is faithful and just and will forgive us our sins and purify us from all unrighteousness. (1 John 1:9)

Forgiveness, a Gift for the Taking

A few years ago I heard a speaker who came to campus whom I will never forget. Her name is Dr. Mary Poplin, and she is a professor of education at the Claremont Graduate University. She came to faith in her forties while teaching as a radical feminist professor. After accepting Christ as a result of encountering Him in a dream, her life changed dramatically. This included her becoming grieved over two abortions she'd had earlier in life. It was on this journey in faith that she wrestled with repentance and accepting forgiveness from God. She shared that she was at a conference retreat for healing about three years into her walk with the Lord when she was asked by the priest to write on one side of a card the names of people in her life she needed to forgive; on the other side of the card she was asked to write down things in her life for which she needed forgiveness.

Dr. Poplin said that while she was walking with her card, she heard a stern male voice say, "Who are you not to forgive someone I have forgiven!" She heard God say this three distinct times. She was confused. Dr. Poplin dropped to her knees and pleaded, "Lord, I don't know what you are talking about." The response came back, "I forgave you the first time you asked, and I don't want you to ask again." That's when she realized that God was speaking to her about the issues of her abortions.

Dr. Poplin continued:

> A lot of people say to me, "God was telling you that you need to forgive yourself." He actually wasn't telling me to forgive myself. He was telling me You don't even have the authority to do that. Self-forgiveness is something contrived out of secular-psychology. Scripture never asks someone to forgive themselves. In fact, I spent a year reading the Bible looking for any reference to God asking someone to forgive themselves. I couldn't find anything. We are asked to forgive others who trespass against us, and we are asked to go to God for forgiveness, but we are never asked to forgive ourselves. Before receiving this revelation, Scripture had assured me that I was forgiven, yet I was still trying to work it off until I felt that I might deserve it. But trying to "work it off" I would feel free one moment and not the next.

Forgiveness comes from God, and so does freedom. If you don't feel free from past sins, then it's not a matter of self-forgiveness but the fact that you don't truly believe that God is full of grace, mercy, and forgiveness. You don't truly believe that God has forgiven you. Because *if God has forgiven you, who are you not to walk in freedom?* God has all the authority to forgive you, so if He has forgiven you it's sinful for you to walk in unforgiveness, placing your authority over His. It communicates that your unforgiveness is stronger than God's forgiveness. Dr. Charles Stanley has also warned of this spirit of unforgiveness by saying:

> If you're holding an unforgiving spirit toward yourself, the truth is you don't believe that God has forgiven you. How can I hold in bondage, anyone that God has set free—including myself? If you think, "I know God has forgiven me, but . . . " Every time you put a "but" behind that, you add one more bar to your own self-constructed prison. Get rid of the bars, break out of the prison. You don't have to be there. But if you choose to be there, nobody is going to break you out of prison. You've got to want out. Don't allow yourself to emotionally adjust to living in guilt or you will become comfortable living under self-condemnation and be too afraid of being set free.

Dr. Poplin closed out the chapel service at Biola University with these closing remarks, which I feel are fitting for forgiveness with missed opportunities as well:

> Don't walk out of here with a burden you have already asked forgiveness for. It is doing nothing but slowing down your destiny. It is the plan of the enemy for you to hang on to things that you have already asked forgiveness for.

It's the devil's lie that we are still guilty. The enemy wants you to hang on to that guilt until it turns into shame and that shame turns into bondage. The devil wants to keep you from the truth that God

Himself proclaims in Jeremiah 31:34: "For I will forgive their iniquity, and I will remember their sin no more" (ESV).

GotQuestions.org does a wonderful job of expanding upon that verse:

> This does not mean that the all-knowing God forgets because He forgives us. Rather, He chooses not to bring up our sin to Himself or others. When our former sins come to mind, we can choose to dwell upon them (with the resulting guilty feelings), or we can choose to fill our minds with thoughts of the awesome God who forgave us and thank and praise Him for it (Philippians 4:8). Remembering our sins is only beneficial when it reminds us of the extent of God's forgiveness and makes it easier for us to forgive others (Matthew 18:21–35).

One final question you must truly consider is this: "Does the blood of Jesus cover some sins or all sins? – The answer is, of course, all sins. It doesn't matter how big, how small, or how many. All sins are covered and forgiven because of Jesus' blood on the cross" (Todd White).

Transformational Grace

Dr. Charles Stanley points out that many people think, "How can I accept that God has forgiven me when I know that I am going to commit that same sin again?" Dr. Stanley replies, "How many sins did you commit before Jesus died on the cross? None. God forgave you of all your sins before you committed a single one of them." *It's important to note that while God's grace covers all sin, God's grace is not a license to sin. Jesus' power on the cross didn't just cover our sin; it gave us the power to conquer sin. We have Christ in us through the Holy Spirit, which covers sin, conquers sin, and allows us to overcome sin.*

In regard to missed opportunities, salvation and sanctification (progressive holiness) in Christ allow us to move through each stage of life connecting with more and more divine opportunities and missing fewer and fewer opportunities. The life of faith is not stagnant. The power of Christ is not stagnant. The power of Christ and the Holy Spirit can do nothing other than transform, redeem, and change. It's not in their nature to do anything other than transform. If you have received the Holy Spirit, there is no way you can continue to spin your wheels in the same sin. The power of the Holy Spirit gives us the necessary traction to get out of the biggest ditches and holes in life. *If you have persistence in the Holy Spirit, you are promised progress in life. And that progress will always lead you to looking more and more like Christ.*

Let's be clear: while God's grace covers all sin, it is not a license to sin. We have Christ in us through the Holy Spirit, and His presence covers sin, conquers sin, and allows us to overcome sin. But while God forgives the sin, He doesn't always eliminate the consequences. This is why it's important to take this chapter in context with chapter 3: "You are the Answer to Prayer." We must keep in mind that our disobedience to God is not a neutral act. When we are disobedient and miss opportunities, other people's lives are impacted by the consequences. We may repent and be forgiven, but that doesn't apply a magic eraser to the resulting consequences in our lives or those of others.

The fact that our disobedience has consequences is the reason we must remain sensitive to the touch, nudging, and prompting of the Holy Spirit. Even when we miss opportunities, the Holy Spirit is at work in the good grief we feel, so that we will quickly identify the miss, turn to God, and make it right. Below is another story we received from a reader of the *Divine Opportunity* book. Gary in St. Louis, Missouri, got in touch with me to share this wonderful missed opportunity turned divine appointment. His experience highlights how quick repentance, God's grace for second chances, and being a second-time listener can save us and others from unnecessary consequences of disobedience.

> This particular experience involves an elderly couple who lives directly behind us in our neighborhood. This couple is in their eighties and has lived in the house for over thirty years. We've known this couple for a while, and often I will go over to their house to help with things that come up. Most recently, I went over there to help with branches that had fallen down from their tree. The husband, Rich, has been very sick for the past

three years. For the majority of those three years, Rich has been mostly in bed. Since Rich didn't want to go to the hospital, his wife, Ruth, has had to do the caretaking and looking after him for all that time.

Most recently, I intended to go over to their house to talk with them about how things were going. When I called Ruth, she said that she wasn't feeling very well but that I could come over. As I went into their living room, it was just Ruth. Rich really hasn't been able to make it out of his room to make an appearance in quite some time. But as I got there I asked Ruth if I could pray for her health, and I did. She seemed very appreciative of that.

Then I asked how Rich was doing. She said that he wasn't doing very well and was resting. It was then that in my spirit I felt like I needed to go and pray for Rich. I assumed he was sleeping and that I shouldn't bother him, so I let it go. So we talked and hung out for a bit, and then I headed back home. When I left, I just had this feeling that I should have prayed for Rich. I felt like it was a missed opportunity.

At this time I was in a small group at church that was reading the *Divine Opportunity* book. I was more alert than ever to these divine opportunities and missed opportunities, and I knew this was a missed one. When our group met that week, I shared with everyone my prayer time that I'd had with Ruth, as well as my missed opportunity with Rich. And then God began speaking to me throughout that entire week about my missed opportunity. I'd be thinking about it before I went to bed at night, and it would be the first thought when I would wake up in the morning. "You need to go over and pray for Rich! You need to go over and pray for Rich!" That thought was resounding in my mind.

By that Sunday I was really hearing strongly that I needed to go and pray for Rich, and that his time was short. So I called up Ruth, because I knew that neither of them was a Christian, and I told her, "Ruth, I really need to come over and pray for

Rich. God has really been pressing it upon me to come and pray for him, and that his time is short. Would it be okay if I came over and prayed with Rich?" Ruth said, "Okay, please come over tomorrow around 1:00 p.m."

Of course, I showed up on Monday right at 1:00 p.m., and Ruth greeted me at the door. I told her again, "Ruth, God has been speaking to me that I need to pray with Rich and that his time is short." She said, "Okay, he's in his room. But I do want to warn you that he has been very closed off before about people talking to him about God. I want to warn you that there's a chance he may cuss you out. I just want you to know that going into it." I said, "Okay." And we headed to his room.

We walked into the room and Rich was lying there in bed, and Ruth said, "Rich, our neighbor Gary is here, and he says that God has been speaking to him to come over here and talk with you and pray with you. Is that okay?" Rich said, "Sure. He can come in." So I went up to the bed and he grabbed my hand, and I held Ruth's hand as well. I leaned toward him and said, "Rich, God has really been impressing upon me that you don't have much time left here. I would really like to pray with you. Is that okay?" Rich said, "Yes."

So, I went into this full payer, where I laid out the gospel for him, telling him how Christ, the Son of God, came to earth to die for our sins so that we might be made right with God. That it is through acceptance and faith in Christ that we are forgiven of our sins and welcomed into eternal life. I laid out the whole thing. At the end of the prayer, he squeezed my hand and thanked me for taking the time to come and pray with him. Then I prayed over him and Ruth as a couple as well.

When I left their home, I had such a peace and a release, like a burden had been lifted. I felt this euphoria over having been obedient to God's voice. It truly was amazing. This was all on Monday, and then that Friday I got a phone call and received the news that Rich had passed away. What was interesting was that Rich's nephew had a preacher friend who came over to their house that Thursday evening to pray with him. When the preacher got there to talk with Rich, Rich told him, "Oh, it's okay. My neighbor already came over on Monday and prayed with me."

Well, Ruth ended up telling the preacher how God had really been impressing upon their neighbor to come over and pray with Rich, and she let him in on the whole story. What was interesting was that at the funeral the preacher shared that story with the group. He said, "While I was going over to Rich's house on Thursday, I thought I would be getting there at the last inning, with one final shot to bring Rich home. Come to find out a neighbor had already beat me to it." Well, *I* didn't beat him to it—God beat him to it. It was all because God had been pressing me; He put a great sense of urgency in me, and then I was just being obedient to God.

Initially, I thought I had missed the opportunity, but then God kept prompting me and nudging me and—Wow—what a miracle! It's amazing the impact you can have with a single conversation. And how God never ever gives up on people. He continues to give them chance after chance to choose salvation in Christ, even down to their final breath.

> While no single conversation is guaranteed to change the trajectory of a life, career, or relationship, any single conversation can. (Susan Scott)

I love Gary's example of God's grace, persistence, and patience. We serve a God of countless second chances. That's why the Bible is over a thousand pages long. If God didn't have the grace, mercy, and patience He has, the Bible would be a whole lot shorter. That's why it's funny when people complain about not being able to read the Bible because it's "too long"— like, "Ugh, this Bible is hard to get through. God's grace really drags this thing out . . . " Turns out humans, not God, are the ones who cause the Bible to be so long. We are the ones dragging this thing out. I feel this in my own life all the time. I'm currently sitting on two missed opportunities that need to be made right. Just this morning

I was thinking to myself, "My disobedience and slow reaction time to the prompting from God are really inefficient. Now I've got to use time today to return to the missed opportunities from yesterday."

I'll close this chapter the same way it started, with Jeremiah 15:19: "If you repent, I will restore you that you may serve me; if you utter worthy, not worthless, words, you will be my spokesman." This Scripture became abundantly clear in my research on the topic, for most of the people who have tragically missed opportunities have not only talked about their grief and God's grace but have also gone on to share divine appointment moments of redemption they have experienced later in life. And those who didn't yet have a specific redemptive moment did have confident faith that their moment was certainly coming. This is what the final chapter in this section will focus on: the redemptive moments after missed opportunities, for when we repent God will restore.

> God grant me the serenity to accept the things I cannot change, the courage to change the things I can, and the wisdom to know the difference. (Reinhold Niebuhr)

DISCUSSION QUESTIONS

1. What is one missed opportunity or act of disobedience for which you need to repent and turn to God for forgiveness? Identify it and go for it. Turn it loose and release it to the freedom of God's grace once and for all. As Mary Poplin said, "Don't [leave this chapter] with a burden you have already asked forgiveness for. It is doing nothing but slowing down your destiny."

2. Based on this statement—"My disobedience and slow reaction time to the prompting from God are really inefficient. Now I've got to use time today to return to the missed opportunities from yesterday"—what are some practical things you could do to try to speed up your obedience reaction time to God's promptings?

3. Based on Reinhold Niebuhr's prayer, what is one thing about which you need to ask God to help you accept the fact that you cannot change? What is one thing about which you need to ask God for an increase in courage so that you may actually bring about change? What is one aspect of your life in which you need to ask God for an increase in wisdom?

Go Forth

Consider it pure joy, my brothers and sisters,
whenever you face trials of many kinds,
because you know that the testing of your faith
produces perseverance. Let perseverance
finish its work so that you may be mature and
complete, not lacking anything.
—James 1:2–4

James does a beautiful job of pointing out that even our trials and troubles are an opportunity for great joy. Why? Because those troubles, or in this case missed opportunities, are still opportunities for our faith to be tested, for endurance to grow, and for spiritual maturity to be fully developed. This is what I was most impressed by when speaking with people who'd experienced the most challenging missed opportunities. It seemed as though the more weight of the consequences, the more spiritual growth occurred. In this way, *missed opportunities are not wasted opportunities.* There are lessons of disobedience and life consequences that come from missed opportunities that lead to obedience and behavioral change in the future.

Speaker Todd White referred to moments of disobedience, of falling into temptation, or of doubt as "hiccups." While hiccups may occur, it's important that we "don't live in the hiccup," Todd warns. What he means is that *we must not let a temporary setback become an enduring stronghold.* When people live in the hiccup, they allow an interruption of their faith to hold them in bondage. Romans 5:3–5 and James 1:2–4 remind us that it is not God's design or intent for any of us to be put to shame or held in bondage. God's will for our "hiccup" is that we would repent and turn to Him and allow Christ to work in us to produce endurance, development, and spiritual maturity.

The Bible is littered, from start to finish, with detailed accounts of disobedience, godly grief, heartfelt repentance, God's grace, and motivations for going forth in a new direction of redemption. This is the same message for missed opportunities. Jeremy, the youth leader whose story I shared in chapter 4, "Godly Grief," is the perfect example of this spiritual maturation process.

Jeremy first shared his missed opportunity to meet and connect with a visiting high school student. A month later Jeremy found out that the young man had committed a copycat suicide, replicating the suicide of his older brother exactly one year earlier. Jeremy was convicted that if he had taken the time to meet and connect with this young man, he would have likely learned of the suicide of the older brother. Jeremy said that one of the first questions he typically asks has to do with the student's family and siblings. In that process he would have likely been given an opportunity to connect with this young man about his mourning process and how he was handling the loss of his brother. Jeremy couldn't help but consider the What if . . . ?

Praise God, that's not where Jeremy's story ends. Jeremy went on to experience godly grief and God's grace and carried forward into the future a healthy spiritual mentality. Below is Jeremy's account of his story of redemption:

> A couple of years later, I accepted a position as a youth pastor of a church in Missouri. During that time, as the youth pastor, I found myself in a similar situation as before. I was preparing

for a Wednesday night youth service when I was introduced to a new student. Just as before, I was a little rushed and needing to start the service. But this time I took a moment to introduce myself and get her name. I remember telling her that I was excited that she had come to visit, and I asked her if she would be available for a longer conversation in the coming week.

Praise God, we were able to line up a time to get to know one another. In that conversation I asked about her family and siblings. When I asked about her siblings, she got really quiet. I asked what was wrong, and she said, "My older brother killed himself about eight months ago." Everything just came to a screeching halt for me. I took that really seriously, with my history of the missed opportunity in the back of my mind. That missed opportunity was ringing in my head: "You've already missed one—don't miss another." All those feelings of regret came back, but this time in the form of motivation to do whatever it took not to miss the current opportunity.

This time, with this young woman, I was able to make sure we had as much discussion around the loss of her brother as necessary in order for me to know that she was in a safe emotional, spiritual, and physical place. I was careful to make sure she was properly mourning the loss and moving forward in such a way that she wasn't at risk of taking her own life. Thank God, she was able to get the help necessary to move forward with her own safety in mind.

I couldn't help but stop and think, though, that if I had not been made aware of my earlier missed opportunity, I probably would have missed this one, too. If I had never found out that the young man had committed suicide, I would never have realized I had missed an opportunity or the weighty consequences that can come from missing opportunities. And I probably would have continued to miss more and more opportunities. It was the acknowledgment of the consequence of the missed opportunity that made all the difference. As harsh as it was, and as difficult as it was to handle, it was the reality of the consequence of my missed opportunity that led to a moment of awakening.

For me as a youth pastor this has driven me to be more aware, to take that extra moment to greet somebody who is a guest and could be that divine appointment—you never know. I don't think about my missed opportunity as often any longer. I think the missed opportunity is part of who I am more than it is a conscious thought. It has become part of my spiritual DNA, part of how I act and react in life. I have an enduring mentality to make the most of every opportunity, every relationship, every encounter. I know that's a lot to expect of yourself, but I hope that's how I operate.

I try to think about my life from a larger perspective and then try to make a conscious effort, if it's possible, to live with that missed opportunity in the forefront of my mind without having some sort of guilt complex and being weird about it. But there are definitely moments when I have that missed opportunity come to mind as a reminder that this current moment is an important one. So on Wednesday nights, as a youth pastor, I try to meet every new kid who walks into our building. To shake their hand, ask them where they go to school, how old they are, and where they live. By asking these questions I'm hoping that if there is something going on that God will say "This one!" And that I'll be sure to connect with that person on a deeper level. There's no doubt that I operate differently in those moments now.

Let's Get Meeked

Blessed are the meek, for they shall inherit the earth. (Matthew 5:5 ESV)

You might be thinking, "What on earth does being meek have to do with missed opportunities for divine appointments?" Well, this will be quite the segue, but hang with me—it will be worth it in the end.

Recently I read two commentaries on Matthew 5:5 that have forever changed my understanding of what Jesus meant when he said, "Blessed are the meek, for they shall inherit the earth." Sam Whatley provides some initial clarification as to the original defining intent behind the word "meek."

> A casual reading of these verses today would give you a mental picture of meekness that is far from the forceful image common in the Bible times. Our dictionary defines meekness as, " . . . easily imposed upon, submissive, spineless." But wait a minute. Once you realize that this word is a translation of a Greek military term, you get a completely different picture.
>
> The Greek word "praus" (prah-oos) was used to define a horse trained for battle. Wild stallions were brought down from the mountains and broken for riding. Some were used to pull wagons, some were raced, and the best were trained for warfare. They retained their fierce spirit, courage, and power, but were disciplined to respond to the slightest nudge or pressure of the rider's leg. They could gallop into battle at 35 miles per hour and come to a sliding stop at a sword. They were not frightened by arrows, spears, or torches. Then they were said to be meeked.
>
> To be meeked was to be taken from a state of wild rebellion and made completely loyal to, and dependent upon, one's master. It is also to be taken from an atmosphere of fearfulness and made unflinching in the presence of danger. These stallions became submissive, but certainly not spineless. They embodied power under control, strength with forbearance. When Paul speaks of the " . . . meekness and gentleness of Christ . . . " he is describing this kind of obedience.

Colin McIntyre adds to Sam Whatley's analysis by stating, "It is the meek, Jesus said, who would inherit the earth. And this is the sort of life that does not timidly endure, but wreaks havoc on the kingdom of darkness." I love how both Whatley and McIntyre break down and correct the common contemporary understanding of meekness. With the original intent for being "meeked" in mind, one can see the power that can spill over into our daily divine opportunities.

Think of it this way: prior to being saved and accepting Christ, we are like those wild, rebellious stallions on the mountain. Once we have accepted Christ, been born again (John 3:3–8), God begins to train us for spiritual warfare (Ephesians 6:11–17). In that process God places within us His fierce spirit (1 Corinthians 6:19–20), virtuous courage, and spiritual power (Ezekiel 36:26–27). As 1 Corinthians 4:20 states, "for the kingdom of God is not a matter of talk but of power." However, this particular brand of power is different from worldly power. It's not wild, self-indulgent, self-centered, free-wielded power. It's power under control. It's God's power, under God's control. To reiterate, "to be meeked was to be taken from the state of wild rebellion and made completely loyal to, and dependent upon, one's master." In this process we are disciplined to respond to the slightest prompting of the master. Thus we exercise power and courage at the direction of one master.

Martin Collins adds, "True meekness is always measured by Christ's meekness." As you look at the life of Christ, you will see that he had only one master, one voice that he listened to and followed strictly! Jesus' record of this is abundantly clear in John: "Very truly I tell you, the Son can do nothing by himself; he can do only what he sees his Father doing, because whatever the Father does the Son also does. For the Father loves the Son and shows him all he does" (5:19–20). "I do nothing on my own but speak just what the Father has taught me. The one who sent me is with me; he has not left me alone, for I always do what pleases him" (8:28–29). "I did not speak on my own, but the Father who sent me commanded me to say all that I have spoken. I know that his command leads to eternal life. So whatever I say is just what the Father has told me to say" (12:49–50).

Jesus' life is the gold standard for being meeked—completely loyal to, and dependent upon, one master! Jesus was disciplined to respond to the slightest nudge from His Father. If followed, the training process that results from missed opportunities leads us to becoming meeked to the Father. Through the disciplining process of godly grief and the redemptive process of God's grace, it is possible for us "to be taken from an atmosphere of fearfulness and made unflinching in the presence of [social] danger" (Sam Whatley).

The problem many Christians face is that they cannot say with any level of certainty that they listen only to the voice of the Father and do and say only that which the Father tells them to do and say. *Unfortunately, most Christians are schizophrenic; they entertain a multitude of voices in their head from social media, celebrities, news, friends, family, etc. This ultimately keeps them from being completely loyal to God as they allow the competing voices to battle against God's commands.*

Jesus had an intimate relationship with His Father and would reject the voice of the stranger. This is exactly the level of discipline we need to get to when it comes to divine promptings and following through on divine opportunities. When you have an intimate relationship with God and are engaged in reading His Word, you will most certainly be able to distinguish the voice of the Shepherd and respond to His slightest nudge (see John 10:1–16). But as long as you are entertaining a multitude of other voices, you will indeed find yourself struggling in your confidence in hearing from God and responding in obedience to His promptings.

Being meeked is a process of relinquishing over to the Lord full decision-making power in your life. It's the process of discerning the sound, style, and prompting of His voice and responding immediately with full obedience to even the things that seem to contradict your feelings and challenge secular living. The only voice we must listen to and follow is that which is presented to us in Scripture. Any other voice that counters or contradicts the voice of God we must identify, rebuke, and discard. When you do so, you will actually experience a tremendous amount of freedom. Learning to listen to and respond to only one voice will provide you with freedom and direction, preventing you from listening to a multitude of voices that will drive you crazy and send you chasing after the wind.

If any of you lacks wisdom, you should ask God, who gives generously to all without finding fault, and it will be given to you. But when you ask, you must believe and not doubt, because the one who doubts is like a wave of the sea, blown and tossed by the wind. That person should not expect to receive anything from the Lord. Such a person is double-minded and unstable in all they do. (James 1:5–8)

Savior AND Lord

This is so important that I'll reference the Blackabys' position on disobedience once again:

If you have an obedience problem, you have a love problem. . . . There are two words in the Christian's language that cannot go together: "No, Lord." If you say "no," He is not your Lord. If He is your Lord, your answer must always be "yes." . . . When God invites you to join Him and you face a crisis of belief, what you do next reveals what you believe about God. . . . What you do—not what you *say* you believe—reveals what you really believe about God.

Dallas Willard put it this way: "People live what they truly believe. The genuine beliefs of a person are made obvious by what they do."

As Vance Havner has pointed out, it's amazing how many people will accept Christ as Savior but not as Lord. However, *when you merely accept Christ as Savior, you are attempting to claim grace without guidance.* When you have accepted God as Lord over your life, it would be absolutely foolish not to be obedient to His every command. The Blackabys note that "Love for the Lord = Obedience to the Lord." However, it's vital to keep in mind that *Christianity is not a constant state of proving your love for God but a constant state of being in love with God.* There's a huge difference between the state of proving your love and that of being in love. It's a struggle to act out of a place of trying to prove your love to God. It's easy when you're acting out of a place of being in love with God.

To clarify, it isn't like sitting on pins and needles to ensure that you won't miss an opportunity to be obedient. It may feel overwhelming for you to hear constantly from God and perform His every move perfectly. This is not the case, however. God has made His ways known in Scripture. As you read Scripture, you learn to recognize and internalize the voice and intentions of God. It's not at all about being in a posture of fear that your every misstep could somehow thwart the will of God. That's just not the case. *Allowing God to be Lord is more like a loving marriage, where you already know what your spouse would prefer; it's just a matter of choosing to honor their desires over your own when they conflict.*

> *Meekness* is a real preference for God's will. Where this holy habit of mind exists, the whole being becomes so open to impression that, without any *outward* sign or token, there is an *inward* recognition and choice of the will of God. God guides, not by a visible sign, but by *swaying* the judgment. (A. T. Pierson)

Below is a divine opportunity example from my friend Julian Lowe, someone who has truly been meeked in his walk with God. Julian will listen and respond to God's slightest promptings, even when they seem absolutely crazy. But his experience over the years has taught him that God is worthy of trust and obedience, even when it requires entering a conversation with so many unknowns.

I was at Starbucks with my assistant going over my calendar for the coming month when I looked up and saw this twenty-something girl sitting across the way. She was wearing headphones and working on her computer. When I saw her, I asked God, "Why am I noticing her?" That's when I heard God: "I want you to go over there and say to her, 'Runaway.'" My first thought was, "Nope, not a chance." I mean, come on, I'm a forty-year-old black man. I can't just roll up on some girl in a Starbucks and say to her 'Runaway.' That's creepy." So, I just ignored it.

As we continued on with charting out the monthly calendar, I just kept getting this sense that I needed to go over to her and say to her "Runaway." Honestly, I kept hoping that the prompting would just go away. But the longer we sat there and talked, the stronger the feeling got. Again, I'm thinking, "How in the world can I possibly approach this twenty-something girl with this in a way that isn't completely creepy?"

As we finished up, I was still extremely hesitant and holding out hope that the prompting from God would go away. So we packed up and started walking toward the door to leave, but I still couldn't shake this feeling. In fact, I started to get that churning in my stomach that I needed to be obedient or I would be missing something.

So I took a deep breath and walked over to this young woman. I leaned over, put my hands on my knees, and tried to look as polite and innocent as possible, knowing what I was about to say to her. As I leaned in toward her, she pulled her headphones up, gave me a bit of an annoyed look, and said, "What?" I said to her, "Sorry to bother you, but I'm a pastor in LA. And this is going to sound weird, but as I saw you sitting over here from across the way, I got this feeling that God wanted me to come over here and tell you, 'Runaway.'"

She said, "Oh, my gosh, I just got chills." I asked, "What? What does 'runaway' mean?" She replied, "Well, I have these three best friends in the entire world. And they are the only three people who know me and call me by the nickname 'Runaway.'" I stood there for a second, just blown away. Then I said, "Well, I think God just wants you to know that He knows you even more intimately than those friends, but He wants that level of intimate relationship with you that you have with those friends."

When you've been meeked and made completely loyal to and dependent upon one master, it's amazing the work you will see God do in your life. God prizes loyalty and obedience over all else. Even the most talented, gifted, brilliant people will not see the fruit of God in their life unless they are listening intently to His voice and are willing to be obedient to His commands—even to the seemingly craziest of thoughts and ideas. *Loyalty and obedience will take you farther in life than any amount of talent or giftedness.*

Side note: With all this hearing from and being obedient to God discussion I want to be sure to include a caution from Dallas Willard:

> When God speaks to us, *it does not prove that we are righteous or even right.* It does not even prove that we have correctly understood what He said. The infallibility of the messenger and the message does not guarantee the infallibility of our reception. Humility is always in order.

Further, when we do hear from God and share that message with others, we must be sure that it does not contradict the Word of God. It's also good practice to encourage the recipient of the word to pray over it and let God confirm it for them as well.

Focus on the Calling, Not the Gifting

> It's not about gifted or ungifted, it's about those who give themselves versus those who withhold themselves. (Martin Buber)

Henry and Richard Blackaby, in their book *Experiencing God*, point out that too many people focus on the gifting rather than on God's calling. They insightfully note that we must reverse this order and instead focus on the calling and trust that God will equip us with the needed gifting:

> If God merely provided us with a gift, we would tend to place our confidence in the gift rather than in Him. But since the Holy Spirit does the

work through us, we must continually rely upon our relationship with Him if we are to be effective in the ministry He gives us. Conversely, if we refuse to obey what God asks us to do, the Holy Spirit will not equip us. *We don't need to be equipped for something we refuse to do.* Our divine enabling always comes as we obey what God tells us to do—never before our obedience. (emphasis added)

I love that line "We don't need to be equipped for something we refuse to do." I truly want you to understand that it is not at all about being gifted or ungifted, which is how the vast majority of people view divine appointments. Most people think, "The people who have these amazing stories have something different that I don't have." That may be true, but not in the way you would expect. Because it's not a particular giftedness these people have; it's obedience, courage, and a willingness to allow awkwardness for God. *God can do more with the ungifted-obedient than He can with the gifted-disobedient.*

Think about my friend Julian; it wasn't his giftedness that allowed for that amazing moment with that young woman "Runaway" at Starbucks. It was his obedience, courage, and willingness to allow for awkwardness. And it resulted in a moment that would have been completely unexplainable were it not for the presence of God in his and her lives. There is something transformational that happens inside you when you realize that there is no other way to explain what took place other than the presence of the Holy Spirit in your thoughts and words. *When you act in your own gifting, you get the credit. When you act with the Holy Spirit's equipping, God gets the credit.*

The people who have experienced the more recognizable missed opportunities are typically the most motivated to make the switch from being worried about their gifting to focusing on their calling. The people who have experienced the weight of missed opportunities are no longer worried about gifting but about the consequences and grief that may come from their disobedience. *These people have developed a powerful one-two punch of love for God and fear of consequences. Their desire to avoid experiencing grief and negative consequences has become more powerful than their desire for certainty and giftedness.* It was the difficult missed opportunity that led them to the realization:

- I'd rather experience a little social awkwardness than a whole lot of grief.
- I'd rather disregard political correctness than disregard the prompting from God.
- I'd rather stumble through a divine appointment than miss another opportunity.

No Leftovers

For me personally, it's not that I walk around all day worried about all the worst possible outcomes of my disobedience, freaked out that each person I talk to is suicidal, dying of cancer, or one car accident away from death. That obviously is an unhealthy way to walk through life. Instead, I'm at a place where I'm in love with God, in love with hearing from God, and wanting others to know how much God loves them, too. As a result, I want to be intentional to go forth with the opportunities I have each day to edify those around me in a godly manner.

I seek to maintain a level of spiritual discernment throughout my conversations, so that I can *be listening to God while listening to others.* When you are regularly reading the Word of God and spending time in prayer, you will *develop a level of spiritual discernment that will keep you from making a conversation more than it's meant to be—but not less than it could be.* The last thing I want to do is go through life with a series of underwhelming conversations, leaving behind a wake of unintended consequences of my disobedience.

My motivation is not to leave any conversational leftovers. I realize that this is an unrealistic goal, because it's a fine line between making a conversation more than it's meant to be and making a conversation less than it could be. Again, *the situation need not be pressure filled, for God makes His intentions clear to us through that still, small voice in our heart. When it's present—I listen. When it's not present—I just enjoy the conversation.*

However, when I do recognize that I have accomplished less than what God had in store for a passing conversation, if possible I do what I can to follow up with the person. The story below is an example of a time when I quickly recognized that God had more in store for a person than I had originally communicated and shared with them. After these types of conversations, I feel a check in my spirit, a caution flag that signals to me that there was more God wanted to communicate to the person.

> One Friday, I was at the dentist office for a regular check-up. When I went in it was just myself, the receptionist, and the dental hygienist. We had the usual introductory conversation, and then I lay down in the chair as the hygienist, Lupe, prepared for the cleaning. It was then that she asked, "So, what do you do?" I told her, "I'm a college professor over at Azusa Pacific University." She said, "Isn't that the Christian college?" I replied, "Yes." She asked, "What do you teach?" I replied, "I teach Communication. Overall, I teach students how to develop emotional intelligence so they can better develop, engage, and sustain relationships—romantic, family, and work relationships." Lupe asked, "How do you teach that in a Christian way that's different from any other university?"
>
> I thought, "Wow, how do I answer that in under a minute, before these utensils start being shoved in my mouth?" So I quickly said, "Well, essentially the difference comes down to the value of life and treating people like sons and daughters of a living God. And the Bible speaks to so many Truths about relationships and communication that are backed up and supported by the most contemporary secular research."
>
> Then came the poking and prodding of the dental cleaning. At that point it was primarily Lupe talking as I answered the questions the only way dental patients can, with "Uh huh" and "Un uh." But Lupe went on to talk about how it must be challenging for biology professors and others to teach from a Christian perspective. (She assumed that science is at odds with Christianity, which it isn't. However, this comment would later make more sense.)

Lupe ended up having to numb half my mouth for a deep cleaning, so at this point I was pretty much strictly a listener in this ongoing conversation. She shared, "A couple of weeks back, I was watching a debate online between Bill Nye, the Science Guy, and a Christian scientist. Bill Nye ended up winning the debate; it was kind of sad. But the years that Bill Nye laid out for the formation of the world, from the scientific community, weren't matching up with the estimations from the Bible. Anyway, it was interesting to hear the two of them debate."

Of course, I was just listening and making random noises to let her know I was listening, but I was incapable of actually talking. Lupe continued on with the cleaning and conversation, which eventually moved around to other topics. When it was all said and done, half my mouth was numb, the other half was agitated, and I was sent over to the receptionist to pay for that beating she had just given to my gums. I felt as though I should say something to Lupe before leaving, but I had no idea what to say or whether I was even capable of having a conversation with a numbed mouth. So I simply said goodbye and headed out to my truck.

When I got in my truck to leave, I immediately got the sense that I still needed to say something to Lupe. I got that check in my spirit that God had more in store for her. So I sat there for a minute trying to pray and figure out what I could possibly go back inside to say. I prayed and received just enough to awkwardly start a conversation and see where it would go. I got out of my truck and walked sheepishly back into the dentist office. The receptionist asked, "Did you forget something?" I said, "Actually, I just had something to share with Lupe. Is she still around?" She said, "Yeah, hang on a second."

Lupe came walking up to the waiting area and opened the door. I said, "Hey Lupe, when I got in my truck to leave, I thought more about what you said about Bill Nye, the Science Guy, winning the debate based upon the scientific years and dates. I felt like God wanted me to tell you that He is not the least bit concerned about Bill Nye, the Science Guy, and his dates. Those scientists' years and estimations change every couple of decades anyway as new science emerges. And while the scientists are constantly changing with time and technology, God is still the same yesterday, today, and forever. And for God a day is like a thousand years, and a thousand years are like a day. And most importantly, God doesn't care about dates—He cares about relationship. He cares about having a personal relationship with you."

Lupe replied, "Thanks for sharing that. It's a good reminder." I said, "Is there anything I can pray for you about?" She asked, "Why? Do you think I need prayer?" I said, "Well, everyone could use prayer for something." She thought about it for a few seconds. Finally she said, "I guess you could pray for my family situation." I said, "If you don't mind my asking, what's the situation?" Lupe said, "Well, my parents don't really agree with some of the life decisions I've been making, and so they recently kicked me out of the house." I said, "I will absolutely pray for that."

So, on that Friday morning in the doorway of the waiting room in a dentist office, I prayed for Lupe that God would give her wisdom to navigate her choices, decisions, and family dynamics. I prayed that she would connect with God and establish a personal relationship with Him. Then I said, "Thanks for letting me share that with you and letting me pray with you." We said goodbye, and I headed back out of the dentist office for the second time, but this time with a sense of peace that I had finally gotten around to sharing what God was calling me to.

As Christians, we can't live in fear of political correctness, social rejection, or the judgment of others. We must be meeked by, with, and for God. As Colin McIntyre states, "It is the meek, Jesus said, who would inherit the earth. And this is the sort of life that does not timidly endure, but wreaks havoc on the kingdom of darkness." We must bear light everywhere we go—edifying, encouraging, and lifting people up. Let us leave behind a trail of blessings from our conversations throughout our day. And should you miss an opportunity, seek God in prayer and circle back around so that person has the opportunity to feel the love of Christ.

DISCUSSION QUESTIONS

1. In what way would your life change if you were to be fully meeked—completely loyal to God, fully under the control, guidance, and direction of the Father?

2. What is the difference between Christ being your Savior and Christ being your Lord? In what ways could you grow in your full acceptance of Christ as Savior? In what ways could you grow in your full acceptance of Christ as Lord?

3. What is the risk of focusing too intently on a gifting rather than on a calling?

Go and Give
Opportunity

Defy the forgettable flatness of everyday work
and life by creating a few precious moments.
—Chip and Dan Heath

At the end of the first Gospel account, Matthew (28:18–20) records
what we now know as the Great Commission:

> Then Jesus came to them and said, "All authority in
> heaven and on earth has been given to me. Therefore
> go and make disciples of all nations, baptizing them in
> the name of the Father and of the Son and of the Holy
> Spirit, and teaching them to obey everything I have
> commanded you. And surely I am with you always, to
> the very end of the age."

I'll be honest: up until a few years ago I viewed the Great
Commission as an overwhelming burden. When I would come across
the Great Commission, I would think to myself, "That's why I tithe! So
we can get those missionaries out there to make disciples of all nations.
I'm just glad they were commissioned and not me—what a bear of
a lifestyle that would be. Yikes." But then, in a conversation with
my father-in-law, David, he paraphrased the Great Commission and
brought it down to my level. He said, "*The Great Commission can be
boiled down to this: Go and give opportunity for people to experience God.*"

The moment he said that, the Great Commission went from being
an overwhelming burden overseas to being achievable and within
arm's reach. "Go and give opportunity for people to experience God,"
I thought. "I can do that." David went on to point out that one of

the most important things you need to remember when it comes to the Great Commission is the difference between your job description and God's job description. Your job description simply includes *giving opportunity* for people to experience God. It's in God's job description to bring His glory and transformation. *We are to present opportunities, and God is to provide the results.* How, when, where, and with whom God chooses to provide or withhold His glory is entirely up to Him. As long as we are providing people with opportunities to experience God, we can walk away with our heads held high, regardless of the results (as long as we are using the Bible as our frame of reference for how to provide those opportunities).

> A wise [person] will make more opportunities than [they] find. (Sir Francis Bacon)

Time to Play Offense

To provide a little background, I grew up playing soccer and basketball, but something shifted in me mentally around middle school when I lost confidence in playing offense and began to focus more on playing defense. In some ways that worked out fine, as I went on to win defensive awards in both sports. Yet in other ways my loss of confidence resulted in my not having the gumption to take the necessary shots or even put myself in a position to have the opportunity for those shots. Additionally, I felt that lack of self-confidence spill over into my personal life. Rather than tackling goals or objectives with full confidence, I would stick to the safer bet; I would wait for opportunities to come my way rather than going out and making opportunities of my own.

Over the past two years, after having been baptized in the Holy Spirit, I have felt God convict me with the thought, "Ryan, it's time to stop playing defense by merely protecting your faith. It's time to start playing offense and giving others an opportunity to experience their own faith. Now is the time to go out on offense and live the Great Commission. You've been playing defense your entire life, not because you lack the talent to play offense but because you lack the confidence.

You must abandon your fear of failure and go out on offense for Jesus and give opportunities for people to experience God."

What I've realized is that the Great Commission is our calling to play offense. It's to actively go out into the world to give opportunities for people to experience God. On a simple, accessible level, the Great Commission is accomplished through a series of divine appointments. Divine appointments break down the Great Commission into achievable and meaningful moments that bring about discipleship in the process.

Playing Offense with Minimum Offense

> We should be leaving behind a trail of blessings
> and healings. (Reinhard Bonnke)

Much like the experience I had with David paraphrasing the Great Commission, I had a similar aha moment upon hearing Shawn Bolz' paraphrasing of divine opportunities: "*It's as simple as calling out the gold in people. Just ask God about His heart and desire for others.*" The moment I heard that I thought, "Calling out the gold in people. I can do that." After all, calling out the gold in people is as simple as reminding them of their original value—they're made in the image of God. It's reminding people that they are a son or daughter of a living God. As Dan Mohler says, "Christ didn't die on the cross for us just because we were sinners. He died on the cross for us because we were lost sons and daughters." Boldly call out the gold in others and remind them of their original and redeemed value as a beloved son or daughter of a living King.

If we can avoid positive withholds (Les and Leslie Parrot describe positive withholds as times when we have something positive to share, like a compliment, prayer, encouragement, or notion of gratitude, and we keep it to ourselves; more on this to come) and instead share all gold—edification and encouragement—with as many people as possible, we *give the Holy Spirit an opportunity to parlay those positive sentiments into divine appointments*. If we do, we'll be blown away with how God goes about using those positive sentiments at just the right time with just the right person. *The only difference between that moment being an encouragement and its being a divine appointment is the presence and work of the Holy Spirit.* Our job is to provide opportunities for people to experience God. It's God's job to bring His glory and transformation.

By approaching divine appointments as *opportunities to call out the gold in people, we exercise the ability to play offense with minimum offense (a minimal possibility of offending).* The first "offense" is that of engaging another person with the intent of providing opportunities for them to experience God. The second "offense" has to do with what we need to avoid: causing annoyance or resentment. If we are engaging in divine opportunities in which we seek God's heart and desire for people and we freely share those positive, encouraging sentiments with others, there will be connection without annoyance. It will leave people feeling blessed and not irritated.

A YouTube spiritual mentor of mine, Todd White, has touched the lives of thousands of people for Christ with a very simple opener for each conversation. Todd begins the majority of his conversations with, "You're amazing! Jesus loves you so much!" Then he proceeds to call out the gold in people with all sorts of positive sentiments, affirmations, and reminders of their original and redeemed value before finishing those interactions with prayer. When was the last time you saw someone get annoyed after receiving a bunch of affirmations and being lifted up in prayer? You will find that to be unbelievably rare. By approaching divine appointments as *opportunities to call out the gold in people, we can take advantage of the ability to play offense with minimum offense.*

> The Sovereign LORD has given me a well-instructed tongue,
>> to know the word that sustains the weary.
>> He wakens me morning by morning,
>> wakens my ear to listen like one being instructed.
>> The Sovereign LORD has opened my ears;
>> I have not been rebellious,
>> I have not turned away. (Isaiah 50:4–5)

I truly believe that we can leave behind a trail of blessing and healing everywhere we go. Calling out the gold in people leaves a trail of blessings. Ministering to the pain in people through prayer leaves a trail of healings—emotionally, spiritually, and/or physically. Everyone has a cross to bear and a burden to carry; there are no exceptions. Anyone who has a pulse has a prayer request. By meeting people where they are in life, seeing their need, communicating with compassion, and through prayer calling God into action—people will have the opportunity to feel blessed or healed. At a minimum they will feel seen, heard, and cared for, and their burden will feel lightened. At a maximum, they will be fully healed by the miraculous salvation of Jesus.

I'll close with this incredible excerpt from Daniel Kolenda's book *Unlocking the Miraculous through Faith and Prayer*:

> By this definition, God in all His splendor, can and does move into the natural realm of human existence where He can actually be experienced by people. I believe that people everywhere long to be touched by God in a tangible way. A lost and dying world longs to see the gospel, experience the gospel, and be touched and healed by the power of the gospel. They want to do more than just hear the gospel with their ears. **A person who hears the gospel should have an experience that needs an explanation, not just an explanation of something that is in need of an experience!** The gospel must be a life-altering encounter.

This final section of chapters is meant to provide you with some tangible ways to begin giving opportunity for others to experience God. I believe you will find these chapter instructions to be practical, relatable, and within arm's reach. The point of this is to get the ball rolling, experience some small wins, grow your confidence, and increase your trust in God. I pray that you will not be just a hearer of divine appointments but become a doer. In becoming a doer, you will leave a trail of blessings and healings everywhere you go. And from this trail of blessings and healings will emerge a powerful personal testimony of God working in and through you.

DISCUSSION QUESTIONS

1. How did this opening section cause you to think differently about the Great Commission?

2. A message from the chapter was: "Your job description simply includes giving opportunity for people to experience God. It's in God's job description to bring His glory and transformation." In what ways is that more motivating than the reverse: "It's in God's job description to give opportunity for people to experience Him. It's in your job description to bring His glory and transformation."

3. Identify one person who stands out in your mind as someone who plays offense with minimum offense. What is it about their style of sharing faith with people or praying for people that makes them relational and comfortable to be around? What about them or their style of communication could you try to adopt for yourself?

Practicing Courage in Christ

Courage is . . . mastery of fear, not the absence of fear.
—Mark Twain

Perhaps one of the best illustrations of mastering fear is a young David going off to fight the great Goliath in 1 Samuel 17. In this depiction we read about Goliath, the giant Philistine champion, talking all sorts of trash against the Israelites. Goliath challenges any Israelite to a one-on-one fight. Winner takes all. Losing side becomes slaves to the winners. At this time David is still just a boy balancing two jobs. One job playing the harp for King Saul. The other shepherding his father's sheep and running errands for his father and brothers. One of those errands was to take ten loaves of bread and ten cuts of cheese to his brothers on the battleground and come back to his father, Jesse, with a report.

While dropping off the bread and cheese, David hears Goliath taunting the Israelites and "defy[ing] the armies of the living God" (1 Samuel 17:26). This is where we get the phrase "cheesed off" because David was fuming with righteous anger and threw down the ten cuts of cheese to go fight the Philistine. I'm kidding. I'm not sure where that phrase comes from, but it seems fitting.

> David said to Saul, "Let no one lose heart on account of this Philistine; your servant will go and fight him."
>
> Saul replied, "You are not able to go out against this Philistine and fight him; you are only a young man, and he has been a warrior from his youth."
>
> But David said to Saul, "Your servant has been keeping his father's sheep. When a lion or a bear came and carried off a sheep from the flock, I went after it, struck it and rescued the sheep from its mouth. When it turned on me, I seized it by its hair, struck it and killed it. Your servant has killed both the lion and the bear; this uncircumcised Philistine will be like one of them, because he has defied the armies of the living God. The LORD who rescued me from the paw of the lion and the paw of the bear will rescue me from the hand of this Philistine."
>
> Saul said to David, "Go, and the LORD be with you." (1 Samuel 17:32–37)

After that we read about David rolling out with nothing but his shepherd's staff and sling, like a boss. It takes him one shot with his sling to take down the giant, and the rest of the Philistine army turns and runs for their lives. I love it. Every time I read about the life of David, I discover something new. In my latest reading of this story, I discovered two keys to David's success in mastering his fear that I believe are applicable for conquering our fears when it comes to divine opportunities.

First, David practiced courage in smaller battles so he would be prepared for the larger ones. David didn't start with the warrior giant; he had practice with lions and bears. And who knows, perhaps even before the lions and bears he had practice with wolves. Perhaps even before the wolves he had practice with raccoons . . . The point is that you don't just wake up one morning and take on a giant. In Luke 16:10 Jesus points out, "Whoever can be trusted with very little can also be trusted with much." The same goes for taking on lions and bears and Philistine giants. The same goes for divine opportunities.

You need to be faithful with the smaller divine opportunity conversations God places before you; then you will be prepared to be faithful in the larger ones. You must practice courage and accrue some small wins that build your confidence and prepare you for the bigger steps of faith. So don't be discouraged if you don't yet have a list of wowing divine opportunities of your own. Those will come in due time as you begin to step out in faith and practice courage in the smaller conversations of everyday life. This process of practicing courage can often resemble the progression of planting seeds, watering seeds, and being a part of God's increase. If you are faithful in planting and watering seeds in other people's lives, it will only be a matter of time before God uses you as His vessel to bring about growth. (You can read more on that specifically in chapter 11, "Some Plant, Some Water, and God Makes Things Grow," in the *Divine Opportunity* book.)

The second, and most important, key to David's conquering his fear was his track record with God's provision. David knew that it was the Lord who had rescued him from the claws of the lions and bears, and David trusted that the Lord would also rescue him from the Philistine. David approached Goliath with the kind of confidence that comes only from walking with God and having a track record of seeing God's glory and victory in one's life. Todd White refers to this as "Godfidence." *When you have a track record of firsthand experiences with God, your faith and confidence grow as your fears and worries wilt.* Then you're ready to take on even larger victories for the Lord. *The confident expectation of a big win with the Lord comes from a track record of small wins.* When your divine resume includes going after lions and bears, with the Lord's protection catching them by the jaw and clubbing them to death, that's when others will consent and say, "All right, go ahead. Take on the giant."

To recap, there are two keys to David's success in conquering fear that we can apply for conquering our fear in situations of divine opportunity. First, David practiced both courage and skill. He was able to stretch his courage comfort zone and build confidence in his skill set by practicing along a progression in terms of degree of difficulty. Second, as David practiced both courage and skills, he experienced God's faithfulness and presence in the process. He realized it wasn't about his operating in his own strength and skill but that he was collaborating with God in the process. God was working in and through David's steps of courage, and David's confidence grew and grew.

What might that look like for you? Who are your racoons, wolves, lions, bears, and giants? Which communication skills are necessary and needed that you should be practicing and developing? In doing so, you will be prepared when God calls on you to face some giants. And you can face those giants with boldness and confidence because you have a track record of God's provision in the small wins that has developed a confident expectation for the big wins. In the section below and the chapters that follow, I am going to provide you with some practical steps for engaging in this process. So buckle up and get ready to practice some courage.

Exposure Therapy

Exposure therapy is a practical and applicable way of explaining the incremental growth process David experienced in his walk with God and in mastering his fear. Exposure therapy details the process people can take toward conquering anxiety, phobias, and fears. Using this method, therapists have their clients create a *fear hierarchy* that ranks their fears according to the degree of severity. Then they begin the process of incremental exposure, beginning with mildly or moderately difficult exposures and then progressing to harder ones. This is accomplished through a gradual progression of practicing courage.

This can be boiled down to a simple practice for engaging in more comfort zone-stretching divine opportunity experiences as well. This is crucial because the devil toys with our boundaries in many areas of life, expanding some and shrinking others. The devil works to expand boundaries in the area of immorality, loosening us up to be comfortable with increasing amounts of immoral thoughts, words, and behaviors. The devil also works to shrink boundaries in the area of divine appointments, significantly reducing the number of people and places we feel comfortable speaking up on God's behalf. The enemy has constricted many of us to a social comfort zone that doesn't go beyond the phone in our hand. It's time to expand that social comfort zone back out and obliterate those boundaries and restrictions in the name of Jesus!

For starters, you can take some time right now to apply exposure therapy to your personal anxieties or worries about divine appointment conversations. You can begin with a list of fears. The fear list will look different for each individual, depending upon your baseline levels of introversion or extroversion, social skills, tolerance of uncertainty, comfort level with spontaneous face-to-face communication, ease in talking about God, and other factors.

Consider your mild, moderate, and extreme fears and worries when it comes to face-to-face divine opportunities. (You can also reference chapter 6, "Conversational Barriers," in the *Divine Opportunity* book.) This could include ***emotional fears*** in areas such as conflict, embarrassment, criticism, rejection, or judgment. It could also include fears of having a lack of communication skill or a lack of knowledge about the faith. For you personally, what are the exact emotional tensions or triggers at play that might keep you from engaging in a divine-opportunity conversation?

You might also create a list of the types of ***people*** with whom you might have an easier or harder time discussing elements of faith and list them in an increasingly stress-inducing order. For example, do you have an easier or harder time bringing God into conversation with younger people, people of your own age, or older people? How about strangers, acquaintances, coworkers, friends, or family members? How about people of various ethnicities or socioeconomic status? As you sketch out your mild, moderate, or severe people-related fears, you can look for individuals in the mild or moderate grouping to start practicing courage.

Then create a list of the types of ***topics*** you have an easier or harder time discussing with others in terms of faith. Some people have an easy time offering prayer for others but a difficult time asking someone about their relationship with God. Others have an easy time talking about God in a broad sense but struggle with talking about Jesus. Still others have an easy time talking about God's blessings but a hard time talking about life's struggles. Again, sketch out the mild, moderate, or severe faith-based topics you might struggle with discussing, matching this list with that of the types of people with whom you might feel most comfortable in such a conversation. This will give you another list of topics and people in the mild or moderate grouping from which you can start practicing courage.

The final category in which to create a list has to do with the *situations or settings* in which you are likely to have an easier or harder time discussing your faith. Some people have an easy time talking about their faith in their church's small group session but a hard time discussing their faith at mixed dinner parties. Others have an easy time talking about faith in one-on-one settings but struggle in groups. Others have an easy time talking about faith at friends' homes but struggle with similar conversations at their workplace. Still others have an easy time acknowledging Jesus at youth group but would never dare mention His name at school. Coordinating these lists will give you a final set of situations in the mild or moderate category from which you can start practicing courage.

Once you have thought through your emotions and fears regarding divine opportunities with various people, topics, and settings, you're ready to begin practicing courage. Again, the beginning point will vary depending upon your baseline levels of faith, communication skills, and overall ease with divine opportunities. You can feel free to start with any of the following three scenarios: (1) imagined exposure, (2) video modeling or mentor modeling, or (3) real-life exposure.

(1) Imagined exposure. You probably already started this process when thinking about your emotions, people, topics, and settings, above. However, a great first step is to engage in the process of *imagined exposure*. This is where you will stop and think vividly about the people, topics, and settings that bring on in you mild, moderate, or severe emotional reactions. Next, you can pick a person, topic, and setting in which you would like to grow in terms of your level of comfort when engaging in divine opportunities. Then you can use vivid mental imagery to place yourself in the scene with this imaginary person and play out some possible scenarios, exchanges, and alternative responses they might have to your questions, comments, or conversation starters.

The more you do this, the more real the situation becomes, and the more mentally and emotionally prepared you will feel when you find yourself in those divine situations in the future. Just keep in mind that the nature of conversation is naturally impromptu, so one can never fully predict what to expect. However, imagined exposure will at least give you some sense of familiarity as a starting point.

(2a) Video modeling. This is something that has helped me tremendously. Video modeling is a process of watching someone else model your desired behavior. As you watch the video model with enough repetition, you will begin to feel comfortable practicing similar behavior in real life.

In the last few months I have been watching Todd White on YouTube as he goes around talking with strangers on the street and praying for physical healing. Todd has provided great video modeling for me and has given me a place to start in terms of how to begin conversation, questions to ask, and ways to approach prayer. If you YouTube "Todd White praying for healing," two things will happen: (1) you'll be blown away by the power of God working through Todd's obedience, and (2) you'll be challenged to grow in your expectation of God's movement. Through his videos he has certainly expanded my comfort zone and willingness to pray for healing.

The key to video modeling is that you need to find someone who will stretch your comfort zone in a relationally achievable way. I really appreciate Todd's relational and casual approach with people, and his communication style seems to be within the reach of my own abilities. There is no sense attempting video modeling of people who are way beyond your zone of intelligence, communication, or style. That will be more discouraging than motivating. Spend some time searching YouTube with an eye open for people who would be appropriate models for you. Then begin practicing courage.

(2b) Mentor modeling. If you can't find someone on YouTube who's an appropriate video model for you, then find someone from your church, in your family, or as a part of your friend group who might be a good model of faith conversations and engaging with divine opportunities. Then hang around that person as much as possible and observe them in action. Listen to how they start conversations, make transitions, ask intentional questions, and extend opportunities for prayer. The more you see and hear others doing this, the more comfortable you will become with doing it yourself.

I have had the opportunity to observe my father-in-law, David, in action multiple times. This has given me a chance to see him interact with people and have a specific model to operate from in terms of his approach, communication, posture, questions, comments, transitions, segues, and closing remarks. He has been a great example for me to follow and model myself after. I have used portions of his questions, commentary, and closings in various conversations of my own. However, there are other aspects of his personality and style I cannot mimic, and if I did it would probably come off as awkward and weird—the point here is that we need to use discernment. After all, he's a jolly, grandpa-aged pastor who can get away with saying and doing things that a 38-year-old cannot. So find those video or personal models in your life, observe them in action, make note of the attributes you feel comfortable with in terms of your personal and relational style, and then put them into practice. You'll be surprised how effective this can be.

(3) Real-life exposure. The final step is going out and practicing courage. Pick out some people, topics, or settings that fall into the mild to moderate side of your fear spectrum, and then start praying for divine opportunities and guidance and start talking to people. You have to begin somewhere, sometime, with someone—so why not now? *There is too much brokenness, sickness, and loneliness in this world for us to waste another day not knowing who we are in Christ and not walking in all we are called to be in Christ.* Let's get after this thing. Every day we pass people who are hungry for relationship, thirsty for connection, and sick of being ignored. The soil is fertile and the harvest is ripe, so let's stop wasting time and letting ripe fruit rot on the tree simply because the workers are too few. (For more practical insights, you can reference the additional strategies listed in chapter 8, "Optimistic Obedience," in the *Divine Opportunity* book)

Practicing Courage

I'm going to walk you through my recent journey with practicing courage and give you some specific examples on how to proceed. There are two areas in which I have been trying to stretch my comfort zone, step out in faith, and grow in spiritual maturity. The first is praying for people's healing. The second has to do with sharing thoughts of divine encouragement with people over issues God puts on my heart and in my mind.

Healing prayer. Lately I've been challenged to be praying for people's physical healing when needs arise in conversation. I'm not talking about writing down the prayer request, taking it home, and putting it underneath my pillow at night. I mean, in the moment, asking them if I can pray for them, and then lay a hand on them and pray for Jesus to heal them right then and there. Since doing some video modeling of Todd White on YouTube, I have taken several steps to practice courage:

Step one: I began praying out loud for my own knee, which needed healing. I'd had constant, nagging issues with my left knee for the past four years, to the point at which I couldn't even do a full squat without it hurting. It was hard to even pull my left leg back to stretch my quad without the knee hurting. I haven't had full range of motion in my left leg for all of that time. After a couple of weeks of praying out loud over my knee, I began to see improvement and healing from my four-year lingering injury. I now have full range of motion and mobility.

Step two: I began praying for my kids and my wife's healing when sickness or injuries would occur. I did this enough that my kids began to model after me. Just this past week I got a bad 24-hour bug and got really sick, and my seven-year-old son came over and said to me, "Dad, I'm going to pray for your healing." Then he laid a hand on me and began to pray for healing in the name of Jesus. A few weeks before that, our one-year-old tripped, fell, and bumped her head, and our five-year-old daughter walked by her, touched her on the head, and said, "Be healed in the name of Jesus." Then she went over to the table and went right back to working on her craft. What's really awesome is that when we take steps to practice courage it becomes contagious with those around us. Without even realizing it, I had become the model for the rest of my family.

Fast-forward six months. My wife was at the church worship practice before a service when one of the singers opened up for the first time about chronic back pain she has been dealing with for a long time. Another singer suggested, "Who wants to pray for a miracle?" My wife responded, "I will!" So she prayed for her to be healed. And sure enough, God did a miracle and healed this young woman of her chronic back pain right then and there.

Step three: we went over to a friend's house for one of their kid's birthday parties, and when I got over there I noticed that my friend was wearing a medical boot on his left foot. I asked him what had happened, and he shared that he had sprained it really badly playing basketball. He wasn't sure whether it was fractured or sprained or to what degree. In the midst of the party, I felt as though we should all stop and pray for him, but I withheld because I felt awkward doing that at a birthday party. I missed the opportunity. However, a day later I texted him to ask if I could come over and pray for his ankle. This friend is a Spirit-filled believer, so this wasn't out of the ordinary, but it was still a stretch for me. The day after that I went over to his house and we prayed over his ankle; we rotated between praying and having him test out his ankle to see whether there was any healing. Unfortunately, there was no miracle that day, but I know he appreciated the fact that I went out of my way to pray for him.

Step four: I recently hosted a Night of Gospel, Comedy, and Justice for a nonprofit called Reach Up Reach Out that serves widows and orphans in Uganda. At the end of the event, people came forward for prayer. The first person to come to me was this twenty-something young woman named Kaylee. She said she had been suffering from migraines and asked if I could pray for healing. So I set off in prayer and thanked God in the mighty name of King Jesus for healing this young woman! After the prayer she stepped back, rolled her head around, and said, "You know what, by the time you finished praying I realized that I couldn't feel any pain anymore. God healed me!" Praise God! Praise God! Praise God!

The journey of praying for people's healing continues, and I'll be real—it's still hit or miss, but we are seeing people get healed. What motivates me is a simple vision of dying and standing before God in all His glory. The second I see Him in all His majesty and radiance, I immediately realize how much more could have been accomplished in His name here on earth had I just had the faith, love, devotion, and boldness. What if we actually believed that the Lord our God is indeed God, Creator of the heavens and the earth? What if we started acting like we were saved? What if we walked with Godfidence, knowing that the Bible is TRUE!?

I recently asked a group of students, "How many of you believe that God can heal people?" The entire class of twenty-three students raised their hands. Then I asked, "How many of you in the last month have laid hands on someone and prayed for their healing?" Only three hands remained in the air. Well, here's the harsh reality. If you say that you believe God can heal people but never pray for anyone to be healed, there are only two logical reasons. One, you don't actually believe God can heal people, or two, you're the cruelest person on the planet. Think about it. If you say you believe God can heal people, but then you see someone hurt, injured, or sick and don't lay hands on them and pray, that's cruel. It's time to put your faith to the test. Get out there, start stretching your comfort zone, and begin to lay hands on people and pray for their healing.

Divine encouragement. In the past year I have begun a process of praying for God to give me divine words of encouragement for people. Here's what this journey has looked like for me. When I have time, I try to spend about twenty to thirty minutes in prayer, asking God whether He has a word of encouragement for anyone. Then I try to clear my mind of all the clutter and distracting thoughts. I tell God, "I don't want this to come from my flesh. I want this to come from Your Spirit." I don't want it to be just a word of encouragement from me; I want it to be a word of encouragement from God. This means it will likely include thoughts about this person that I wouldn't have naturally come up with on my own.

This has taken me on a journey of sharing some awesome and some awkward moments with people, and I wouldn't trade those experiences for the world. This too has been a process of practicing courage and stepping out in faith. It's safe to assume that when we ask God if He has a word for anyone the answer is going to be YES! There's not a scenario in which I can imagine God answering, "Nope, not today. There's no one who needs a word of encouragement and no one I want to speak to today." That's just ridiculous. It's safe to assume that God has a word for someone every day, if I'm able to clear away the clutter and take the time to receive it. It's never a matter of God not speaking; if anything, it's a matter of me not hearing.

> **Step one:** a little over a year ago, I was praying before taking my son to school and I simply asked God, "Do you have a word for anyone today?" After I had cleared the clutter of my mind and rested in silence for a bit, the crosswalk lady who works at the corner of the intersection at my son's school came to mind. I didn't know her name or anything about her at this point. Then I asked, "God, what do you want her to know?" Again, as I cleared the clutter and sat in silence, some specific thoughts of encouragement came to mind. This was something I wouldn't personally have desired to tell her. But the thoughts that came to mind seemed to fit with the biblical call to edify and build others up, so it seemed that something divinely appropriate would be encouraging for her to hear.
>
> After dropping my son off at school, I said a quick prayer and asked God for courage and good timing to be able to have this conversation. As I walked back around the sidewalk, I saw her standing there talking to another woman. Unfortunately, it looked as though this was a conversation that wasn't going to be wrapping up anytime soon, and I still needed to get to work. The two women were both in their mid forties and appeared to be friends.

I walked up and said, "Excuse me. Sorry to interrupt, but I had something I wanted to quickly share with you." She replied, "Sure, what is it?" I said, "This may sound a little awkward, but earlier this morning I was praying and asking God if He had a word for anyone today, and you came to mind." She said, "Really?" I continued, "Yes, and in that prayer I felt like God wanted me to tell you that He loves you so much and is so proud of you. God wanted me to remind you that what you do here at this corner of the intersection is so important to Him. He has blessed you with a wonderful smile and a friendly demeanor, and He loves seeing you smile, talk with, and encourage others here every morning. While this may sometimes feel like a small role or small corner of the world to you, it's an important one in the eyes of God. There are hundreds of people who cross your path every day, and you have the honor of greeting them, smiling at them, and encouraging them. You absolutely bring life change to this intersection, and you need to be encouraged and reminded of the great, godly work you do here. God loves you, and He's proud of you."

As her eyes began to get a little watery, she said, "Thank you so much for sharing that with me. That is so encouraging. I believe in God, and I'm glad you shared that with me. Not too many people would have the courage to share that with a stranger. And if God ever puts me in your prayers again, please be sure to let me know." Then the woman next to her chimed in, "That was one of the sweetest things I've heard."

Since that day I've found out that her name is Jenny, and we have occasionally kept in touch when I happen to see her around the school.

Step two: about two months ago I was writing a chapter in this book from a Starbucks near campus. As the end of my time there was wrapping up, I stopped and prayed, "God, before I leave here, do you have a word for anyone?" Again, I had to take several minutes just to clear away the clutter and feel as though I might be able to hear from God and avoid the thoughts of the flesh. After several minutes, the barista at the register came to mind, so I asked, "God, what do you want her to know?" Again, several thoughts of encouragement came to mind that were not things I would have naturally desired to share with her.

When this happens, it's almost as though my own thoughts have cleared away and the thoughts I am having are now coming from God. This particular thought included a word of knowledge about her life—how her family of origin hadn't provided very good parenting or a warm family dynamic, but that God was going to redeem that in her life. This increased the risk of potential awkwardness, but if from God it would also increase the spiritual reward for this barista. The barista, Sierra, was a twenty-something young woman with tattoos along her arm; she was very bright, encouraging, and friendly with all the customers.

Before packing up my stuff, I prayed, "God, if this is from you, I am willing to take the risk, but I need you to bring this Starbucks to a screeching halt so I will have the time for this conversation with her." When I packed up my stuff and got ready to leave, I looked over to check the length of the line. Sure enough, there was no one in line. Then I looked out at the drive-through kiosk, and no one was in line there, either. This in and of itself was a miracle!

So I thought, "Here we go!" I walked over as she was filling up the ice bin and said, "Hi, I was just wondering if you had time for a quick conversation?" She said, "Sure, what is it?" The two of us walked down to the side away from the register, and I said, "This might seem a little random, but I was just praying and I felt like God wanted me to come over here and encourage you. First, I see the way you are always so encouraging with each customer and how much you care about people, so I wanted to encourage you. I felt like God was prompting me that He is going to use your encouragement and care for people to open doors for you in your future employment. That you are going to receive promotions and experience movement up into more and more management positions because God knows He can trust you with His sons and daughters and intentionally place people in your care.

"Second—and this is going to seem a bit random—I wanted to ask you about your family growing up. How was your family dynamic, and how were your parents?" Keep in mind, I was pretty nervous at this point, because I had no idea how a barista was going to respond to this in the middle of her shift. But she immediately jumped in and said, "Well, I didn't really grow up with a dad. My dad left when I was at an early age. My mom raised me, but she hasn't always been the most supportive. She later got remarried to a small, quiet man who was also emotionally distant. So my family dynamic wasn't very good or very supportive."

To me, her immediate willingness to answer and go right into her story was confirmation that this was a divine opportunity and that the word of knowledge about her life was on target. I replied, "Well, here's what I felt like God told me when I was praying—you can take it or leave it, but God wants you to know that He is going to redeem that in your life. God has an incredible family in store for you, and you are going to be an amazing mom. What you lacked in your past God is going to redeem in your future. You don't need to worry about it; it's going to happen for you. Because marriage and family are things a lot of people your age worry about: 'Am I going to meet my future spouse, what will they be like, and am I going to have a family?' You don't have to worry about that, because God has that in store for you. You can just enjoy life, continue to encourage others, and follow God and let Him take care of the rest."

Sierra replied, "Wow, thank you so much for sharing that with me. Not a lot of people would have had the courage to share that. That's so amazing. I do believe in God, but I am still walking through that. Really, my mom is not encouraging it. Any time I tell her I am going to church she makes fun of me. This is really encouraging. Can I give you a hug?" I said, "Sure, can I pray for you?" She replied, "Absolutely. Do you want to hold hands?" So here we were off to the side of the register at Starbucks, holding hands and praying for God to continue to do a mighty work in her life and continue to reveal Himself to her. Right as I ended the prayer, she gave me a hug, and customers were now walking through the door. The timing was divine. The word of encouragement had spoken to her heart. And I was filled with so much awe and wonder in this process of being used by God.

Step three: later that same evening as my experience with Sierra, my wife and I were on a double date with some friends. We decided to take the metro train from Azusa to Pasadena for dinner. While we were on the train I noticed this guy seated across from me on the other side of the door. I asked God, "Why am I noticing him?" The thought that came to mind was that he was thinking about his mom. I wrestled with that in my mind for a bit, because it would be awkward to ask someone, "Hey, are you thinking about your mom?" So I was very hesitant.

Then my wife saw me looking at him and asked, "What's going on?" I made a big mistake: I told my wife about the potential "God thought" he was thinking about his mom. The reason it was a mistake is that my wife grew up with a dad who'd had these kinds of divine appointments all the time, so she knows *it's better to be obedient and wrong than to be disobedient and right.* So she said to me, "Well, then ask him."

Now I was stuck, because I either had to face the awkwardness and ask or face being disobedient to the prompting and look like a coward in front of my wife. So what did I do? I found a loophole. I waited until I saw him stand up to get out at the coming exit, knowing that when he went to leave we would have a maximum of twenty seconds of awkwardness before the door would close and we would leave him in the dust at the station behind. This way, if I were wrong we wouldn't have to awkwardly sit next to each other for another twenty minutes until we got to Pasadena. I'm not advocating for this strategy—I'm just being real with where I was at in my spiritual maturity at this time.

Regardless, I decided to practice courage. I figured the worst-case scenario was that it would feel awkward for a moment and then he would be gone, but at least I would get to see if I was right or wrong. This would at least help me grow in my ability to discern these "God thoughts" and realize when I'm on or off track. The doors opened and he went to walk out, and I yelled, "Hey!" He stopped and turned. "Yeah?" I responded, "This is a random question, but were you just sitting there thinking about your mom?" He got a confused look on his face and replied, "Was I just thinking about YOUR mom?" I reply, "No, were you thinking about your own mom?" Then the door started to close, and he had to take a step back before saying "No." Then the train took off, and we did indeed leave him in the dust—probably confused and now wondering about both his mom and my mom.

Hahaha . . . Honestly, I couldn't help but laugh at myself and the whole situation. It was so awkward, confusing, and hilarious all at the same time. But I did practice courage, test the God thought, and grow in my ability to discern the Spirit. I include this story so that you'll know that not every conversation is going to be a win. Some will be awkward, but it will be worth it. Practicing courage comes with risk, yet people's souls are worth it. Remember, you'd rather be obedient and wrong than disobedient and right—and risk learning the lesson the hard way with a heartbreaking missed opportunity that results in tragedy.

Step four: about two weeks ago I was speaking to a local youth group on the topic of romantic relationships. These are always interesting nights because it's really quite awkward and challenging speaking about relationships to a room of about forty students ranging from the sixth through the twelfth grades. That's a significant and important gap in ages when talking about romantic relationships: you've got some sixth- through eighth-grade boys who are not interested and struggle to contain their immaturity for thirty minutes while hearing about relationships. Then you've got ninth- through tenth-graders who are interested but trying to pretend they aren't. You might even have some eleventh- through twelfth-graders who are in the throes of the experience and perhaps have already accrued some relationship baggage they're trying to figure out what to do with.

However, on this particular evening, even before I went up to speak, I had noticed this girl in the group who had blue hair. When I notice individuals in a room, I've gotten into the practice of asking God, "Why am I noticing this person? Is there something you want them to know?" Of course, in this case I was confused as to whether I was noticing her because of the blue hair or because God had a word for her, or both.

So I gave the message. While I was speaking, I did notice that she appeared to be engaged, making eye contact and listening. I was still noticing her but not feeling led to say anything to her in particular. We wrapped up the night, and everyone headed out.

The next morning I got to my office and took some time to pray and see whether God had a word for anyone. During this time the girl with the blue hair came to mind again, along with another girl who had come up to me after the message and told me how much it had impacted her. So I asked God what He wanted them to know. Below is the email I sent to the youth pastor about the words of encouragement I had received for the girl with blue hair.

Pastor,
I felt like I received this word this morning for the girl with blue hair who was sitting a couple of rows back on my right-hand side as I was looking out at the students.

These sorts of messages are still new for me, so not entirely sure how accurate this is since I know absolutely nothing about her other than she has blue hair.

Girl with Blue Hair:

Luke 6:38 Give, and you will receive. Your gift will return to you in full—pressed down, shaken together to make room for more, running over, and poured into your lap. The amount you give will determine the amount you get back.

She has a creative spirit and creative giftings. If and when she gives those creative giftings over to God, fully surrendering her gifting to God, she will receive the kind of blessing Luke 6:38 offers.

God gave her the creative gifting and He wants her to fully trust that gifting to the One who gave it to her in the first place. Her life will be like playing a game of catch, tossing her gifting back and forth with God where she will be collaborating with God. But she can know with confidence that when she relinquishes control by throwing the gifting back to God that He will for sure throw it back to her and it will return with a stronger anointing each time.

God will be her creative collaborator. If and when she does relinquish full control of her gifting to the One who gave it to her in the first place, she will see it return to her in full—pressed down, shaken together to make room for more, running over, and poured into her lap. The amount by which she surrenders her gifting to God will determine the amount she gets back. If she partially submits the gifting to God, she will only receive a partial blessing; by comparison to the kind of full blessing God desires to give her.

I don't know if she plays music or sings, but I got the sense that she desires a place up front either to play, sing, share art, or share a message. But she's hesitant to make the move herself. She doesn't feel qualified or worthy from her personal mindset, but what she doesn't know is that God Himself has already made her worthy and He has already deemed her qualified.

I got the sense that she has a journal, diary, or digital log of writings, thoughts, etc. In that "journal" is all sorts of gold. Thoughts or notes that could be turned into songs, art, or poems. Just in need of surrendering those to God.

She has the favor of the Lord upon her. She may not realize it for herself just yet, but God's hand is upon her. And what I said last night, in particular, pertains to her, that she should never jeopardize her favor with God for favor with man or favor with the world. If she holds tightly to God, even in the hardest of times, she will most certainly see God's favor overflowing and poured into her life.

God is good all the time. God isn't just good when times are good, He's good even when times are hard, difficult, or depressing. God isn't just good when you have a good family and good parents. He's good even when you don't.

God loves her so much and He is so proud of her. And He desires collaboration with her in her life. She must realize that she is already anointed, but it could be years before she recognizes a place of appointing.

Share with her the story of David [this is something my pastor recently pointed out]:

Samuel came along early in David's life and God anointed him as the next king. However, it was 15 years later that God appointed David as king. Like David, she must remain faithful in the time between the anointing and the appointing. The time between the anointing and appointing is where most people grow impatient and jeopardize the favor of the Lord for favor in the world. If she can remain steadfast in the Lord in the time between her anointing and appointing, she will be blown away by what God does in her life. Her patience will reveal God's perfection.

The pastor sent the email to the girl with the blue hair and this was her response: "Wow! That was extremely accurate. Everything made sense and fit perfectly with me. I am honestly speechless."

The pastor also told me that she shared the email with her mom, and her mom cried as she read it. It has become a great source of encouragement to her relationship with God. God is so personal and so GOOD!

The confident expectation of a big win with the Lord comes from a track record of small wins. This has a been a process for me; these experiences and divine appointments didn't come overnight—this has been years in the making as I've grown in intimacy with God and boldness in faith and taken steps to practice courage. The good news is that it doesn't have to take you as long as it took me to get to this point. That's the whole reason for my writing *Divine Opportunity, Untapped Potential,* and *Perfect Peace in the Perfect Storm*: so that I can package together the most practical and insightful lessons I've learned over the years in the hope that you can fast-forward this process of spiritual growth with these divine lifehacks.

At the end of the day, you can't catch a fish if your line isn't in the water. Today is the day to start fishing for people. Start praying for opportunities, seeking divine guidance, and stepping out in faith. Most importantly, just enjoy yourself, enjoy the company of other people, and get into conversation with the heart of God and the desire to encourage. Remember, the goal is simple: *Go and give opportunity for others to experience God by calling out the gold God has placed inside them.*

DISCUSSION QUESTIONS

1. Take some time to think about this concept of divine appointments, maybe even reflect on a few of the stories you have read thus far, and then write down some of the emotional fears that come to mind when you consider divine appointment conversations. Who are the types of people you have an easier or harder time talking to? What are some faith-related topics you have an easier or harder time talking about? What are some situations and settings in which you have an easier or harder time speaking up?

2. Who is a spiritual mentor (friend, family member, fellow church member) you could spend time with to learn from, observe, and watch in action? I challenge you to call, email, or text them right now to line up a time this week to meet and talk. Write down a list of questions you would like to ask them. Start the process of receiving some legitimate spiritual mentoring.

3. What is one actionable step of faith you could take this week in order to stretch your comfort zone for divine opportunities?

Stop Second-Guessing God

God is setting up divine appointments,
and it's our job to keep them.
—Mark Batterson

I recently had a friend, Pastor Julian Lowe, come to my class for a guest lecture. While talking to the students about trusting God, he gave an example I will never forget. Julian said:

> You know, what I realized about human nature is that we put more faith and trust in Uber drivers than we do in God. For example, whenever you get an Uber and the car pulls up, how many questions do you ask the Uber driver before you are willing to get into the car with them? For most people, the answer is zero! The car pulls up and we jump in the back and the driver takes off headed toward the destination. No questions asked; we have complete trust they will get us where we need to go.
>
> I've never seen a situation where the Uber driver pulls up and the person starts asking a bunch of

questions: Can I verify your driver's license is legit and up-to-date? When was the last time you got an oil change? Do you have the newest update on your app in case new routes have been added? Is the prescription for your glasses current? How much tread is left on these tires? Can you pop the trunk so I can make sure there's no dead body in the back?

No, that never happens. We don't ask a single question when it comes to Uber drivers. But if God wants to take us somewhere in life, we've got all sorts of questions for Him. God, what are you doing? Where are we going? Is this the fastest route? Is there an easier path? Can we take the highway so there are fewer stops? Can I check with my pastors, parents, friends, colleagues, and neighbors? And if they all confirm what I'm hearing from you, then I'll just have two remaining questions and I'll be ready to go with you, God.

Does that sound familiar? We've got to learn to trust God and be willing to jump in and go for a ride.

This doubting of God's directives and God's ways is one of the most common things I hear when it comes to missing opportunities. In fact, after I shared about divine opportunities in a theology class, a student, Laura, wrote to me with these comments:

> Our discussion on divine opportunities reminded me that every day as we walk out into our own city, campus, or community we walk out into a mission field. I started praying about that afterwards. Specifically, I prayed that I would experience a divine opportunity. And God actually brought up an opportunity that *Friday!* Unfortunately, I passed it up . . . AHH! I started doubting that it was really from God. So that made me think about my trust in God. Do I believe that God is with me when I interact with someone? It really reflects my level of faith. Also, it reminded me of

the importance of learning to recognize and listen to the voice of God. How do we know for sure that it is God speaking to us?

How Do We Know for Sure?

Laura expressed one of the most common questions I get asked: "How do we know for sure the prompting is from God?" This is a primary concern for Christians—and a legitimate concern. It's wise to check your heart and verify that you are truly acting in the name of God. This is why it's so important to be reading your Bible daily!!! The more familiar you are with God's Word, the more quickly you will be able to recognize His voice and discern His Spirit. As you read your Bible, you see story after story about prophets, disciples, and apostles who could quickly recognize the voice of God and were immediately obedient to His directives. How could they hear and recognize God's voice so quickly and clearly? Because they had close fellowship with God. The closer your fellowship with God, the more quickly and clearly you will recognize and respond to God's voice.

The closer your fellowship with God, the less time you will spend questioning God and the more time you will spend being obedient to Him. Don't get me wrong: checking with God is good practice. Making sure we are hearing God's voice and not the voice of selfish ambition, motives, or desires is healthy practice. However, we tend to take our questioning of the still, small voice of the Holy Spirit too far at times. We tend to overanalyze and ask too many questions about rather obvious divine opportunities before we are willing to move. And as a result, the moment passes us by.

I heard a sermon from Francis Chan in which he described a time when a couple had come to him, saying, "We really want to adopt a child, but we aren't sure this is of God. So we want to take time to pray and see if that's God's call for our lives." Francis looked at the couple and said, "Well, what do you have to pray about? God has already told you to adopt children in Scripture—James 1:27: "Pure and genuine religion in the sight of God the Father means caring for orphans and widows in their distress and refusing to let the world corrupt you." God has already spoken to us all that we are to adopt and care for children. That has already been made clear. In fact, if you want to pick up a widow while you're at it, that would be fine with God, too."

This is the same line of thinking when it comes to people's opportunities for divine appointments. We tend to overanalyze and question rather obvious situations in which God has already spoken to the issue in Scripture. Typically, a student expresses this concern: "I didn't follow through and I let the moment pass, because I wasn't sure if it was from God." I always ask them, "Well, what was it that you felt prompted to share with the person?" To which the majority reply with something along these lines: "I felt prompted to tell them that God loves them." "I felt like asking if I could pray for them." "I felt like encouraging them with a compliment." "I felt like encouraging them in their faith." "I felt like introducing myself and seeing how I could be of help."

I think it's safe to say that all of those prompts are from God. God has already spoken on these issues, directing us to encourage others, pray for others, and share God's love with others. In Romans 12:13 Paul directs, "Share with the Lord's people who are in need. Practice hospitality." And in 1 Peter 5:14 Peter calls on us to "greet one another with a kiss of love." The author of the book of Hebrews puts it this way in Hebrews 13:2: "Do not forget to show hospitality to strangers, for by so doing some people have shown hospitality to angels without knowing it." Once again, this time in 2 Corinthians 1:4, Paul speaks of the God "who comforts us in all our troubles, so that we can comfort those in any trouble with the comfort we ourselves receive from God." In Romans 1:12 Paul expresses his desire "that you and I may be mutually encouraged by each other's faith." And again in Galatians 6:10: "Therefore, as we have opportunity, let us do good to all people, especially to those who belong to the family of believers." In Colossians 4:5–6 the apostle calls on us to "be wise in the way you act toward outsiders; make the most of every opportunity. Let your conversation be always full of grace, seasoned with salt, so that you may know how to answer everyone." And finally, in Colossians 3:16–17, Paul declares,

"Let the message of Christ dwell among you richly as you teach and admonish one another with all wisdom through psalms, hymns, and songs from the Spirit, singing to God with gratitude in your hearts. And whatever you do, whether in word or deed, do it all in the name of the Lord Jesus, giving thanks to God the Father through him."

In fact, God goes on to say that when we don't do these things we are living in sin. When we withhold good from others, it's a sin! Ouch! Sin—really? Isn't that a little extreme? Not if you read James 4:17: "If anyone, then, knows the good they ought to do and doesn't do it, it is sin for them." Proverbs 3:27 makes a similar point: "Do not withhold good from those to whom it is due, when it is in your power to act." We have overcomplicated our calling, and often we let the devil overtake our thoughts in place of God. God has already spoken loudly and clearly in regard to the vast multitude of divine opportunities you might find yourself in. However, we let the devil get into our heads and instead entertain the foolish doubts he lays before us. As a result, *we often become obedient to the doubts from the devil and disobedient to doing the good of God.*

In the book *Experiencing God*, the Blackabys provide a great way to think about identifying the voice of God:

> When the Royal Canadian Mounted Police train their people in anti-counterfeiting work, the trainees don't focus on counterfeit bills. It is impossible to know all the ways to make fake money. However, only one genuine type of ten-dollar bill exists. So, they thoroughly study the legitimate bill. That way, anything which doesn't measure up can be readily identified as counterfeit. The more intimately aware you are of a genuine article, the easier it is to recognize a fake.

The same holds true for Christians: the more you read and study the Bible, and thus the more intimately familiar and aware you are of God's voice, the easier it is to recognize a false word, voice, or temptation. In John 10:2–5 Jesus points out the importance of the sheep knowing the voice of the shepherd:

> "The one who enters by the gate is the shepherd of the sheep. . . . The sheep listen to his voice. He calls his own sheep by name and leads them out. . . . His sheep follow him because they know his voice. But they will never follow a stranger; in fact, they will run away from him because they do not recognize a stranger's voice."

There is no easy route, cheat sheet, or shortcut to knowing the voice of God—you MUST read your Bible.

> You always tend to talk like those that you spend the most time with. If you spend quality time in the Word every day you will indeed start to talk to yourself and others like Jesus! (Pastor Anthony Powell)

First-Time Listeners

One day my son, David, was bugging me like crazy in a ploy to get a toy from Target. But around that same time he was being a terrible listener. The combination of the two was driving me nuts. So I stopped him and said, "David, if you can be a first-time listener for the next 24-hours, one whole day, then I will take you to Target and let you pick out the toy." I stated it that way because I knew for a fact he didn't stand a chance at making it 24 hours with being a first-time listener.

When I walked away from that interaction with my son, I felt God convict me by asking, "Ryan, when was the last time you were a first-time listener to me for 24 hours straight?" To which I replied, "Touché! I see what you did there, God. Well played."

Here's the thing: while first-time listeners are preferred, second-time listeners will do. In Matthew 21:28–32 we read the parable of the two sons:

"What do you think? There was a man who had two sons. He went to the first and said, 'Son, go and work today in the vineyard.'

"'I will not,' he answered, but later he changed his mind and went.

"Then the father went to the other son and said the same thing. He answered, 'I will, sir,' but he did not go.

"Which of the two did what his father wanted?"

"The first," they answered.

I firmly believe that there are many times when the Lord has spoken clearly and we have ignored Him or even dared say, "No, can't do it. Sorry God, that's going to be too awkward." But we need to repent and go! This parable teaches us that, while first-time listeners are preferred, second-time listeners will do. And *it's far better to be a delayed second-time listener than to be a deceptive first-time listener* who says "Yes" but does not follow through.

I had a student, Kyle, who shared a missed opportunity to be a first-time listener:

Over the weekend, I was driving home from work. As I was headed back on the highway, I saw a car pulled over on the side of the road. I immediately felt this prompting to pull over and help. But for some reason, I second-guessed it. And it delayed me just enough to miss being able to pull over and help.

As I drove on, I really felt convicted that I didn't pull over to help and might have missed a divine opportunity. So I pulled off at the next exit and circled back around on the side streets so that I could get back on the highway at a point where I could pull over and help. But by the time I finally made my way back around, it had taken so long that someone else had already pulled over to help. I felt let down because I might have missed an opportunity to be used by God.

I really appreciated Kyle's heart and desire to circle back around and be a second-time listener, and I'm sure God did, too. While first-time listeners are preferred, however, second-time listeners will do. And *God is so gracious to accept our second-time obedience, even though He prefers it to be first-time.* Even in little missed moments like that, Kyle's willingness to respond to the conviction, to turn around and go back, speaks volumes about where he is at with God. Kyle could have brushed off the whole thing and thought, "Oh well, it's too late now. That opportunity has come and gone." Instead, Kyle made the effort to go back for another chance. I believe that Luke 16:10 applies to such moments in life: "Whoever can be trusted with very little can also be trusted with much, and whoever is dishonest with very little will also be dishonest with much." Additionally, *if you are a faithful second-time listener, you are well on your way to becoming a faithful first-time listener.*

After reading the stories in the *Divine Opportunity* book, readers often express how much they would like to experience just one of those types of moments. Well, those life-changing divine appointments don't always happen overnight for people. *The larger divine appointments often come later in life, after people have been faithful to smaller moments first.* When God knows He can trust you to be obedient to His promptings in the small, positive expressions of prayer, compliments, and encouragement, He will trust you to be obedient in the more crucial moments of people's lives.

Positive Withholds

Most missed opportunities come in the form of "positive withholds." As mentioned in an earlier context, relationship experts Les and Leslie Parrot describe positive withholds as times when we have something positive to share, like a compliment, prayer, encouragement, or notion of gratitude, but keep it to ourselves. These make up the vast majority of missed opportunities. I'm sure everyone can think of times when they had a compliment or thought of encouragement, gratitude, thankfulness, or prayer but instead of sharing it with the person kept it to ourselves. That is a positive withhold—a missed opportunity for us to do the good work of God. While positive withholds might not sound like the biggest of problems, they do have the potential to leave behind a gaping hole of missed connection. Here is a list of positive withholds people have shared with me over the years:

- "I wanted to tell my elderly mom how much I appreciated her and how much I appreciated how hard she worked to be such a great mom, but by the time I had that conversation with her she already had dementia."
- "Before my friend moved away, I wanted to tell him how big an impact he had made in my life in terms of how I approach friendships and make myself available for others. I missed an opportunity to do so in person before he left. I ended up texting him this later, but it didn't feel very significant that way."
- "There was a time when I was volunteering when we all made 'essentials bags' for the homeless, but I was too shy to actually give mine away to anyone."
- "I recently had the opportunity to stop and help someone who was crying, but I didn't think I had the time so I didn't stop."
- "Someone asked me how I was doing, and I gave them a generic response, even though I desperately needed someone to confide in."
- "I was in the cashier line at the grocery store when I noticed that the woman in front of me appeared very sad and tired. I felt like I needed to ask and make sure she was okay, but I just kept unloading my cart. She ended up paying and leaving. I then saw her unloading her things into her car in the parking lot, and I felt the need to reach out. But I just kept walking by . . . "
- "There is a girl in my youth ministry who has never really been involved in anything we do. She sits by herself and doesn't really talk to anyone. Recently, we

found out that she is pregnant, and my heart sunk. I wanted her to know that she wasn't alone, and if she ever needed anything she could count on us. One day I saw her sitting by herself at the end of the service, and I had a very clear opportunity to go and talk to her, but I didn't. I turned around and talked to someone else instead."

- "I noticed a student in my class who always seemed disengaged and lonely. I felt like I needed to go and talk to them, but I didn't. Then about three-quarters of the way through the semester that student was murdered."

Wow, aren't those powerful, eye-opening examples of positive withholds! It's crazy what second-guessing God, ourselves, and positive sentiments can rob us of and cause us to miss out on. Recently I heard Andrew Horn, a social entrepreneur, modify the adage "If you don't have anything nice to say, then don't say anything at all." He took that statement and marked out a few words to turn the phrase around: "If you ~~don't~~ have anything nice to say, then ~~don't~~ say it ~~at~~ all." I think there's truth in both of those statements. If you don't have anything nice to say, then don't say anything at all. But if you do have something nice to say, then say it all, and say it right away! Don't accrue positive withholds as missed opportunities. Share those positives with as many people as possible! *Give the Holy Spirit an opportunity to parlay those positive sentiments into divine appointments.* If you do, you'll be blown away with how God goes about using those positive sentiments at just the right time with just the right person.

Brittany, a student affairs professional on a college campus, shared the following divine opportunity that resulted from the expression of a positive sentiment:

A few years back I had trained and prepared myself to run in the Rock 'n' Roll half marathon in Phoenix, Arizona. However, the week beforehand I got really sick. To the point where I didn't think I was even going to be able to participate, let alone be able to finish the race. I kept up on every medication I could in order to try to make it happen. By the grace of God, I was barely in good enough health to attempt to run the race. In response to that, I ended up wearing a shirt that said "Expect the Unexpected." I thought it was appropriate.

Then, as I was running, about midway through the half marathon I came up behind this woman. This all took place in a matter of seconds, really. But as I was running up behind her, I noticed her shirt. She was wearing one of those screen-printed shirts with the picture of a woman and the dates of her birth and death at the bottom. It was clearly a memorial shirt and a celebration of life. But as I looked closer, I realized that the date of death was only two days before the race. I put two and two together that this was likely her mom and that she had so recently passed away. And here she was running in this race two days later.

Then, as I was running by her, the Holy Spirit prompted me, and without even thinking I said to her, "She is so proud of you!" And this woman looked at me and just started crying. It hit me so hard, because the prompt to say this came from Jesus. I never even had a chance to think about saying that ahead of time. It just came out. And I could tell by her immediate reaction that it meant so much to her! And then, as I continued to run on, I started sobbing. It really touched my heart as well. And while it was such a brief moment in time, it's a moment I will never forget because it was done in the power of the Holy Spirit. I just thought to myself, if that was the whole reason for running this race, then so be it.

This is a quick, wonderful story that is also analogous of life in general. It's as though we are all running the race of life, surrounded by thousands of people, and we may or may not recognize anyone's troubles other than our own. *Often we are so focused on running our own race, making our best time, and reaching our own goals that we view other people as an obstacle to avoid, an obstruction to get past, or an inconvenience to sidestep.* In doing so, we never take the time to see them as God's sons and daughters who might just be wearing their troubles on blatant display and needing to hear a kind word, feel a gentle touch, or receive some daily motivation to keep them running their own race.

> People aren't an obstruction, they're an opportunity.
> (Todd White)

Let's stop second-guessing God on what He has already made so clear in Scripture. *Let's let our positive comments run wild and give God a chance.* Let's give the Holy Spirit an opportunity to parlay those positive sentiments into divine appointments. We serve a God of second chances, so should you miss an opportunity to be a first-time listener, repent and go for it! While first-time listeners are preferred, second-time listeners will do!

Unnecessary Testing

When you read your Bible, you start to realize that the true men and women of God were first-time listeners to clear instruction from the Father. There were very few times when these men and women held out questions and tests for God in order to confirm His directives. For these trustworthy and passionate followers, putting God to the test was the exception, not the norm.

One instance in which we do see someone test God is during a dire situation. And even then it is a simple test, followed by immediate obedience. In 1 Samuel 13–14 we read the story of Samuel giving the Israelites their requested king in the person of a man named Saul. Saul takes over Israel as the tension of an impending battle is brewing with the mighty Philistines. The Philistine army consists of "three thousand chariots, six thousand charioteers, and soldiers as numerous as the sand on the seashore" (13:5). How many men does Saul have? Six hundred, including his son Jonathan (13:15). On top of that, the Philistines would not allow the Hebrews to have blacksmiths in order to keep them from making swords and spears. So on the day of the battle none of the people of Israel had a sword or spear, except for Saul and Jonathan. YIKES!

First Samuel 14:1–15 records the rest:

> One day Jonathan son of Saul said to his
> young armor-bearer, "Come, let's go over to the
> Philistine outpost on the other side." But he did
> not tell his father.
>
> Saul was staying on the outskirts of
> Gibeah under a pomegranate tree in Migron. With
> him were about six hundred men, among whom
> was Ahijah, who was wearing an ephod. He was a
> son of Ichabod's brother Ahitub son of Phinehas,
> the son of Eli, the LORD's priest in Shiloh. No one
> was aware that Jonathan had left.
>
> On each side of the pass that Jonathan
> intended to cross to reach the Philistine outpost
> was a cliff; one was called Bozez and the other
> Seneh. One cliff stood to the north toward
> Mikmash, the other to the south toward Geba.
>
> Jonathan said to his young armor-bearer,
> "Come, let's go over to the outpost of those
> uncircumcised men. Perhaps the LORD will act
> in our behalf. Nothing can hinder the LORD from
> saving, whether by many or by few."
>
> "Do all that you have in mind," his armor-
> bearer said. "Go ahead; I am with you heart and
> soul."
>
> Jonathan said, "Come on, then; we will cross
> over toward them and let them see us. If they say
> to us, 'Wait there until we come to you,' we will
> stay where we are and not go up to them. But
> if they say, 'Come up to us,' we will climb up,
> because that will be our sign that the LORD has
> given them into our hands."
>
> So both of them showed themselves to the
> Philistine outpost. "Look!" said the Philistines.

"The Hebrews are crawling out of the holes they were hiding in." The men of the outpost shouted to Jonathan and his armor-bearer, "Come up to us and we'll teach you a lesson."

So Jonathan said to his armor-bearer, "Climb up after me; the LORD has given them into the hand of Israel."

Jonathan climbed up, using his hands and feet, with his armor-bearer right behind him. The Philistines fell before Jonathan, and his armor-bearer followed and killed behind him. In that first attack Jonathan and his armor-bearer killed some twenty men in an area of about half an acre.

Then panic struck the whole army—those in the camp and field, and those in the outposts and raiding parties—and the ground shook. It was a panic sent by God.

I provide this example because it points out several things about men and women in the Bible and their obedience to God, and how that compares to that of today's men and women of God. First, it took a whole 'nother level of faith for the armor bearer to follow someone into an impossible situation when the prospect had been introduced with "*Perhaps* the Lord will help us . . ." If I had been the armor bearer, I would have replied, "I'm sorry, did I catch a 'perhaps' in there? 'Cause I prefer to follow people with a bit more of a sure thing going for them."

Second, Jonathan set up a fifty-fifty scenario! "If they say this, we go. If they say that, we don't." Again, if I had been the armor bearer, I would have said, "Jonathan, how about we test the waters with a scenario that is not fifty-fifty? Let's think of a scenario that is very improbable; if the Philistines confirm it, we'll go. How about if the Philistines look at us and call us by our first and last names and provide the birthdates for all our siblings—then we'll go! How does that sound?"

Third, when the Philistines did confirm Jonathan's test, his immediate response was "Come on, climb right behind me, for the Lord will help us defeat them!" Boom, and they were off and climbing. The Bible doesn't give us indication that there was any hesitation or follow-up test.

The fourth and most important takeaway I hope you catch is this: the times when Old Testament men and women of God put Him to the test before being obedient were situations in which they were faced with seemingly impossible feats or life-altering decisions on behalf of all of Israel. NOT when they felt prompted to pray for someone. NOT when they felt like sharing a nice compliment with a stranger. NOT when they felt like encouraging someone in their faith. NOT when they felt like introducing themselves and asking how they could be of help. In this particular situation, it was when two men, with one sword, were about to pick a fight against an entire army of thousands! That's when they felt the need to double-check with God.

We need to stop second-guessing what God has already made abundantly clear in Scripture: "Therefore let us move beyond the elementary teachings about Christ and be taken forward to maturity" (Hebrews 6:1). I'll end this chapter with a few criteria for evaluating promptings—for those situations when you are wondering "Is this from God?" Quickly evaluate your prompting based on any or all of these five questions:

1. Is it biblical?
2. Is it within the will and character of God?
3. Will it bring glory to God?
4. Will you share it based on pure motives?
5. Will it edify, encourage, and build up this person?
   (1 Thessalonians 5:11)

I hope you noticed a theme here: you have to be familiar with the Bible in order to discern what is or is not from God. READ YOUR BIBLE, people!

In the words of Todd White,

You can be a believer and have God reveal something for you to do and avoid it because you're scared to walk that out because righteousness isn't solid in your life. You're still ashamed of what other people could think, so you avoid stepping into what God has revealed. You become a hearer and not a doer. You look at yourself in the mirror and see Christlikeness and then you walk away and forget who you are [James 1:22–25].

How many people have thought they heard something from God, but were afraid to do it because they didn't know if it were true or not? How are you ever going to know if it were God unless you do it? And what's the worst that could happen? We have limited ourselves in our own small mind because we're not thinking with the mind of Christ, we're thinking with what we've been through, what other people have put us through—that we can't possibly be called to do that. . . . What if it's about Christ in us?

You can be 100% prophetically dead-on every time, when you say,

"I just want to tell you that God loves you so much. You're amazing. He sent his son Jesus to die for you and to give you life and life abundantly."

DISCUSSION QUESTIONS

1. Think of a time when you were a first-time listener to God's prompting in your life. What were the circumstances? What was the prompting? Why were you convinced the prompting was from God? Why did you respond quickly, with trust and obedience, in this instance?

2. Think of a time when you were a second-time listener to God's prompting in your life. What were the circumstances? What was the prompting? Why were you hesitant to respond with trust and obedience? What caused you to question the prompting this first time?

3. What are three positive withholds you have experienced in the past? If it's possible, I encourage you to share the positive withholds with those people right now. You can meet up with them face-to-face, video chat, give them a call, or shoot them a text. Notice that the options start with the most impactful and move toward the least impactful. Personally, I prefer to have conversations face-to-face and then to follow up with an email or text that reiterates what I said so they won't forget. This way they have something to revisit as a reminder of the details of the positive share.

Divine Opportunities Made Easy

Wherever we go Jesus wants to move
through us and flow through us,
He wants to touch the world around us.
—Todd White

One of the first steps toward engaging in your own firsthand experiences with divine appointments is that of noticing people. In order to notice people, first you need to put your phone away. Yep, I said it. Keep your phone from being a false idol in your life and causing you to miss all sorts of opportunities. Put your phone in its proper place emotionally, spiritually, and physically. This means putting your phone in its proper place in your list of priorities, as well as putting your phone in the proper place in your pocket or bag so that people—not your device—become the object of your attention. (You can read additional insights on this in chapter 1, "Open Your Eyes to the Things Unseen," and chapter 4, "Prompted by the Situation," in the *Divine Opportunity* book.)

Don't be a zombie who is emotionally and spiritually dead to the world around you. *Come alive in the Holy Spirit and have a heart for noticing and loving the people God puts in your path.* In other words, act as though you're SAVED, act as though you're a follower of Christ, and act as though you care more about God's sons and daughters than you do about what's happening on social media. When you recognize the fact that all these people around you are equally loved by God, created in His image, and have a soul that is to be cherished, you will begin to see people as opportunities, not as obstacles. For what you do for the least of these, you do for Christ. Conversely, what you don't do for the least of these, you don't do for Christ (Matthew 25:31–46).

> Look for a need and meet it.
> Find a hurt and heal it.
> Be alert to the cry for help and answer it.
> Listen for the voice of God and speak it.
> Identify someone's weakness and overcome it.
> Look for what's missing and supply it.
> When you do, the power of God—
> the energizing, enabling,
> charismatic activity of the Holy Spirit—
> will equip you . . . (Sam Storms)

Once you begin to notice people, take a moment and ask, "God, why am I noticing this person?" Perhaps God will give you something right then and there; then you can move toward starting a conversation, breaking the monotony of small talk, and moving toward more meaningful moments. This process is easier than you might think. And even if God doesn't give you a clear answer to the question of why you're noticing the person, don't just give up and move on. I'm going to give you some specific ways to slide right into divine opportunity territory, with curiosity, to continue to explore what God has in store.

Don't let yourself turn this into a chore or a burden. *When you have the Holy Spirit living inside you and a love relationship with God, divine opportunities are a natural outcome of your daily walk with the people around you.* When you have the Holy Spirit living inside you, you are no longer trying to prove your love for God; you are simply living while being in love with God.

Divine opportunities made easy in three simple steps:
1. The Power of the Prompt to See the Need
2. The Power of Care to Plant the Seed
3. The Power of Prayer to Call God to the Deed

This is not the only way to approach divine opportunities, but it's a great place to start. You could read stories of 100 different divine appointments, and all of them would be unique. Divine appointments are like snowflakes in that no two are exactly the same. However, in my personal experience and research, there are some repeating patterns that we can put into practice. I believe these three steps will be a great launching pad from which to begin the process. The more comfortable you get in engaging with the divine in the day-to-day, the more you can make the process your own. The most important part is taking the models, stories, examples, and approaches from this book and making them your own.

This divine appointment story comes from a former student of mine, Alex, who read the *Divine Opportunity* book when it was published a year after he graduated. Alex was the first reader to send in a divine appointment that was sparked by reading the book. Here you will see how Alex made use of a simple prompt to open up a conversation, dedicated time to the conversation, communicated care, and ultimately ended the evening in prayer.

On Sunday evenings, my church has a service followed by a community gathering time where people can eat, drink coffee, and hang out. It's pretty common for me to hang around for this afterward, as it's a good opportunity to catch up with friends. Usually people stick around and mingle, and pockets of people break off into side conversations.

On this particular evening, I had been there for a while and was getting ready to head out. As I was getting ready to leave, I was looking around and noticed this girl sitting by herself at a nearby table, visibly crying. There were people all around her, but no one was talking with her. I remember hesitating before I left. I had been reading the *Divine Opportunity* book, so I was in the process of noticing more people and more opportunities in the day-to-day. When I saw her, I was surprised that no one else was stopping to talk with her. That's when I knew I had a choice to make to either avoid the situation and head home or go over and talk with her. I knew that by walking away I would be making a conscious choice to avoid her and a potential divine opportunity. Even though I was tired and wanted to leave, I knew I had to go and check on her.

I walked over to the table and asked, "Hi, would it be okay if I sit with you?" She said, "Sure." Then I told her, "I could see that you seemed upset, and I was wondering what was on your mind." She looked up at me and said, "Well, to be completely honest, I'm thinking about committing suicide." I immediately knew this was a divine appointment and exactly where I needed to be. I ended up sitting and talking with her for over an hour as she opened up to me and told me her story. She shared that she had come from a troubled family and that she had been in and out of living situations with different family members, mostly feeling displaced and like a burden to people. She shared that her life had been a series of troubles, one after another, and that she was really struggling. She felt unwanted and unloved and was hurting deeply.

After a while I briefly excused myself just to make someone at the church aware of what was going on, and then I quickly returned to the conversation. When I got back to the conversation, I asked her what her plans were for the night. She didn't share much about her exact intent, so just to be safe I made her pinky promise me that she wouldn't take her own life. It was all I could think of in the moment, but it seemed to work to lighten the mood for a moment and also create a commitment. As we continued to talk, I knew that my job here wasn't complete, so I asked her where she was headed next. She said that she was just going to head home but still needed to figure out a ride. So I offered her a ride home and told her it would give me great comfort just to know she had made it home safely and that her home was safe to go into—which she assured me it was. She accepted the ride home, so we headed out and continued the conversation all the way to her house. Before she went inside, I prayed for her and over her life and situation. Then we parted ways and I entrusted her to God.

The next day I checked back in with pastors at the church to make sure they were aware of the situation, and they followed up with her as well. I've since seen her around the church and had the opportunity to check in with her. Praise God, she's still around and fighting the good fight. And praise God that He put me in her path and gave me that moment to notice her and approach her that night.

As stated in the "Go and Give Opportunity" section, the goal of the Great Commission is simply to go and give opportunity for people to experience God by calling out the gold God has placed in others. *As we move through our day, we should leave behind a trail of people feeling blessed or healed—blessed with encouragement and reminders of God's love for them, or healed from pain, suffering, or discouragement.* The point of these conversations is to "see the need." This is a process of curiosity and discovery. It's caring enough about people to take the time to discover a specific pain-point in their life (emotional, physical, or spiritual), an area of weakness, or a desire for prayer. Finally, it's about ushering in the Holy Spirit through prayer so that people know they have encountered more than just a "good" person—they have experienced God.

The Power of the Prompt to See the Need

A prompt is a question used to encourage a hesitant speaker. Oftentimes, the hardest part of this process is simply starting the conversation or shifting an ongoing conversation out of the mundane and in a direction with meaning. Great prompts have the ability to do just that. (You can read additional insights on this in chapter 8, "Optimistic Obedience," in the *Divine Opportunity* book.)

First, I will preview some prompts you can keep in your back pocket. Then, after I have previewed all three steps, I will walk you through some examples of these prompts being put into practice. Finally, I'll close out the chapter with another real-life divine appointment story that is illustrative of these steps.

Here are a few simple prompts that can spark conversation and put you immediately on the path to see the need.

- "I was just about to sit and pray for my family and friends. Is there anything I can be praying for you about?"
- "On a scale of 1 to 10, how are you really doing?"
- "Tell me about a high point and a low point for you from the past few months."
- "What's one of your biggest hopes or dreams I can be praying about for you?"
- "Tell me about your faith/spiritual journey in this season of life."

You can probably tell that some of these prompts are more appropriate for certain types of people, relationships, and settings than others. This is where discernment and allowing the Holy Spirit to lead you come into play. When used correctly, these prompts will be an invitation for the other person to join you in more meaningful conversation. As you will see below, these prompts can be used in such a way as to immediately put you in a position to see the need.

The Power of Care to Plant the Seed

A kind word seems like nothing, unless that person has not been given a kind word in weeks, months, or even years. (Joji)

Don't just see the need—understand the need and care for it. Don't forget that a storm of silence has swept through this country—in the forms of busyness and technology addictions—and left in its wake fertile soil and a ripe harvest. The best way to plant seeds or harvest the ripe fruit is through genuine care and concern for those around you. People will open up when they know that you genuinely care to hear their responses, needs, and stories. *There are lots of stories but not enough listeners.* Take on the character of God and adopt His heart and desire for people you cross paths with every day. Simply put, care like Christ. When people recognize that you genuinely care about hearing their need and that you have the patience to stop everything else you're doing to listen to their story, you will be blown away by how many will be willing to open up and share with you. *Genuine care and concern plant seeds of love in people's hearts.*

Divine opportunities are unique moments in which we can express nearly all five of Gary Chapman's Love Languages: words of affirmation, quality time, acts of service, gift giving, and physical touch. (1) Words of affirmation are acts of calling out the gold in people—as we freely offer compliments, encouragement, or other positive sentiments. (2) Given how busy and rushed most people are, it takes only a few extra minutes of conversation for some to feel as though they have just received some quality time from you. (3) Amidst the storm of busyness and technology addictions, basic manners of acknowledgment, conversation, and care can truly make people feel as though they are on the receiving end of an act of service. (4) There is always one FREE gift you can give to anyone, and that is the gift of prayer and communion with God. (5) When appropriate, physical touch through a hug at the end of a heartfelt prayer always goes a long way. *When we care like Christ, divine opportunities have the unique ability to communicate love through multiple languages.*

The Power of Prayer to Call God to the Deed

Prayer is a powerful element in this equation for multiple reasons. One, it gives you an opportunity to point to Jesus as the source of your love, care, and concern. If you don't bring God into the equation, others will just think that you're a "good" person, and you will get all the credit. The prayer allows us to usher in the Holy Spirit, recognize Jesus, and call God to the deed. By "deed," I mean action, task, or work. They will know that you care for them out of the love you have received from God, not just because you're a "good person." Many people get rightly upset about people doing bad things in the name of God—like carrying God's name in vain and breaking the commandment not to misuse the name of the Lord. But *I think we should also get upset about Christians doing good things without using the name of the Lord. Too many Christians do good in their own name and get all the credit. This robs God of the glory and robs the other person of recognizing the experience as a divine encounter instead of merely a good encounter.*

Two, by praying and calling God to the deed, you let the other person know that it's not just you who cares about them but that God cares deeply about them and everything they are going through. It's not just about God getting the glory for the divine moment but about God getting to communicate His love for His sons and daughters through you. As William J. Toms has said, "You may be the only Bible some people ever read." *Prayer gives you an opportunity to properly cite the source of your love, care, and concern.*

Three, prayer gives the Holy Spirit another opportunity to speak through you. Just recently I was praying for people at the end of our church service, and my friend Elaine came forward to ask for prayer over a project and direction she was contemplating in her life. I prayed for her and others as the service ended. It wasn't until the next week that I saw Elaine again, and she came over and gave me the biggest hug and told me how much the prayer had spoken to her. She said that everything I prayed was right on point with her life and that the prayer was a confirmation from God on what she needed to do. When she told me this the following Sunday, I couldn't remember anything I had prayed or anything I'd said. It was the Holy Spirit praying through me on her behalf. *When you pray for others, it's an opportunity for the Holy Spirit to communicate through you in a way you would never have been able to communicate on your own in conversation.*

Divine Opportunities Made Easy

Below I will illustrate a few ways you can quickly and easily put these Prompt—Care—Prayer principles into practice. Keep in mind that our goal is to move from the mundane to the meaningful with ease and grace. First we ask an open-ended question to prompt openness. Second, patience and care will draw out the need and allow us to plant the seed. Third, prayer will allow us to call God to the deed and turn things from a merely good conversation into a God conversation.

Just to set the stage, lets imagine a scenario where you walk into Subway to get a sandwich and there is no one else in line. This means you have a little more time to talk than you normally do but not enough for a full therapy session.

Prompt—Care—Prayer #1. I'll begin with the quickest and easiest option. As you are paying for your sandwich, you can ask, **"Hey, I'm just about to sit down, eat, and pray for my family and friends. What could I be praying about for you during that time?"** Give the person some time to think about it. Don't be afraid of a little awkward silence as they stop and think. What they are trying to decide in that moment is whether they want to tell you about their real need or a superficial need. The silence and follow-up in this moment are crucial to let them know you have a genuine desire to hear their prayer request and are serious about praying for them afterward.

Most people will start with a superficial, broad, or generic prayer request. They might say something like "You can pray for my family," "You can pray for success," or "You can pray for a move I have coming up." If they do, you can simply ask, **"Is there anything more specific about that?"** You might have to ask a similar follow-up question a couple of times. As you do, you will begin to hear the real need emerge as the person realizes that you actually care, that they are not an obstacle you're trying to get past, and that you will sincerely pray for their need. They are trying to figure out whether you are the real deal. Your patience in the moment and genuine desire to pray for them will win them over.

When they finally get around to sharing their real need—their real prayer request—you have two options. One, if there is no one else in line, you can say, **"Thanks for sharing. You know what, would it be**

okay if I just pray with you right here?" If it's slow and no one else is in line, odds are they will let you pray right then and there. Boom. Now you can pray over them in person, face-to-face, and make the most of the moment as the Spirit leads you. At the very least, you can pray and close with, **"Thank you for sharing and allowing me to pray. Jesus loves you. God bless."** Then, if nothing else emerges in the conversation, you can go and eat your food. When you finish, you can go over and shake their hand, give them a high-five or a fist-bump, and say, **"Thanks again for sharing. You're awesome. Jesus loves you so much. I'm going to continue to pray for you."**

The second option is that if people are in line behind you and it seems as though it will create an uncomfortable or time-pressed moment for the person, you can say, **"Thank you so much for sharing that. I'm gonna sit down to eat, and I'll be praying for you. Jesus loves you so much. You're awesome. Thanks for sharing."** Then, after you finish eating and praying, you can look for a quick moment to walk over and say, **"Thanks again for sharing. You're so awesome. Jesus loves you. I'll continue to pray for you."**

Prompt—Care—Prayer #2. For this example, lets imagine a scenario in which you cross paths with a coworker or a friend at Target, Walmart, or a grocery store. You can open with, **"Hey, how are you?"** They will likely reply, **"Good. How about you?"** Then you can go right into, **"No, seriously, on a scale of one to ten, how are you really doing?"** I stole this approach from a friend, Julian, who uses it with people at his church. This approach immediately flips a typical mundane interaction in the direction of a meaningful exchange. All of a sudden you've let the person know you genuinely care about how they're doing and are creating a space to hear the truth of the matter.

Most people will give you a quick look of surprise before they stop and actually think about your question. Again, the person is trying to decide whether to open up and tell you the truth or give you a generic answer and get you out of their hair. Your patience and genuine concern will win them over. Most people will think about it and finally give you a number. Some might give you a number and immediately go into a longer response.

If they give you a number only, this is your chance to dig deeper and discover the reason behind the number. If they say a number from zero and two, you might need to clear your schedule for the rest of the day and really invest in that conversation to bring them back to life. However, it's unlikely they will say a number that low.

If they say a number from three to six, you can simply invite, **"Tell me more about that? Why a four—what's going on?"** See how quickly you've moved into seeing the need? Odds are that, if they respond with a number from zero through five, they need healing from some form of physical, emotional, or spiritual pain. This is a chance to lift someone up in their time of need. You'll have to use some discernment and check with the person, but you could either talk with them right there or ask them if you can help them finish shopping and talk in the process and perhaps even pay their bill when they check out (if you can afford it). If it doesn't work out to talk at the store, you can line up a time to connect later, but make sure you set a day, time, and location before you part ways.

If they give you a number around seven or eight, you can still reply, **"Tell me more about that seven."** If they are somewhere around seven or eight, things might be going fine overall, but there is still an opportunity to listen for pain or blessings as they emerge in their response. If they let on about a pain-point or need, you can listen to the story behind that and eventually get to a point where you can ask, **"How can I be praying for you about that?"** Keep in mind that you might need to use the follow-up again: **"Is there anything more specific about that you would like me to pray about?"** After they get around to the full prayer request, you can say, **"Thank you so much for opening up and sharing that with me. I really appreciate it. Would it be okay if I pray for you right now?"** Again, it's always more impactful if you can pray for someone in-person, face-to-face. This sends a wonderful message that you are the real deal, that you care about them, and that you aren't just giving them the Christian brush-off by saying, "Oh, I'll be praying for you" as you walk off into the distance.

If they cite a number around nine or ten, you can still respond, **"Whoa, come on now. Tell me more about that nine."** If they're truly at a nine, life is great, and odds are they're experiencing some big wins and blessings. This immediately puts you in a position to hear what God is up to in their life. You can reply, **"That's incredible. I'm so happy for you. How can I be praying for you during this season?"** There will still be opportunities for prayer, even if it's for their ongoing protection or continued blessings.

The advantage of this approach with the scale of one to ten is that it gives you quick access to the highs or lows in their lives. Either way, it puts you in a position to mourn with those who mourn or rejoice with those who rejoice (Romans 12:15). You have a direct path to identify the needs or the wins in the person's life and leave them feeling blessed or healed. No matter how the conversation goes, you can always find a way to end in prayer and then close with, **"Thank you so much for sharing. You're awesome. Jesus loves you. Just know I'm going to continue to pray for you."**

Prompt—Care—Prayer #3. In this final example, I will address all three of the prompts:

1. Tell me about a high point and a low point from the past few months?
2. What's one of your biggest hopes or dreams I can pray about for you?
3. Tell me about your faith/spiritual journey in this season of life.

The reason for combining them is that these prompts are most appropriate for times of longer conversation with people with whom you have an existing relationship. When that's the case, these prompts are great for moving deeper in conversation. We can all attest to interactions when we've been stuck in a rut, spinning our tires around and around in the superficial elements of each other's lives. These prompts are great for breaking out of the superficial cycle and into a divine territory of conversation.

If you make a commitment to memorizing these three question prompts, I guarantee that you will find plenty of conversations into which to interject them. You don't need to come right out of the gate with these—something like, "Hi, good to see you. Tell me about your faith journey in this season of life! Go ahead. Tell me now. Tell me! Tell me! Tell me!" You don't have to get carried away. But neither do you want to wait too long and throw out one of these questions just as the person is about to leave. Strike a balance. Once you've finished the cordial back-and-forth banter, you can slip into, **"Hey, you know what, I feel a little bit out of the loop with you. What's your faith journey been like in this season of life?"** Or, **"Hey, it's been a little while since we've had a chance to catch up. Do you mind if I ask about a high point or a low point for you in the past few months?"** Or, **"You came to mind recently, and it got me thinking that I don't know what your current hopes or dreams are, and I would love to be praying for you about that. Would you mind sharing?"**

The important thing to remember is that you don't have to feel stuck to a script of any kind. Figure out which questions work for you and your style of delivery. You can also keep in mind that the prompt, care, and prayer do not always have to flow in that sequence. Sometimes people might need to feel your care and concern before they are open to your question prompts. At other times you might be out to eat and have the opportunity to ask about a prayer request before you eat or get into conversation. These prompts are meant to be starting points for launching into more meaningful dialogue, so allow the Spirit to guide you, and use your divine discernment throughout.

> We can't do everything for everyone everywhere, but we can do something for someone somewhere. (Richard L. Evans)

This divine appointment comes from Michele in Florida, who read the *Divine Opportunity* book and shared her own firsthand experience with me. As you read her story, you will see the pattern of prompt—care—prayer threaded throughout:

I received a phone call from my mom late one evening around 11:30 p.m. When family calls you that late, it's not usually a good sign. I picked up the phone and said, "Hey, Mom! Is everything all right?" She said, "No, honey, it's not." My first thought was about my dad, because he had been in and out of the hospital around this same time. I asked, "Is Dad okay?" She replied, "Your father's fine. It's Rachel." Rachel is my niece, who is eight years old. I said, "What's going on?" She said, "There's been an accident. Rachel passed away." I said, "Mom, what could possibly have happened?"

She said, "Rachel was in the backyard playing with her brother and his friends. Her brother and friends were playing on the zipline in the backyard." My sister, Maria, lives in an area of New Jersey where there's a lot of woods and oak trees. The zipline in their backyard had been attached to two of those old oak trees. Apparently, one of the trees was hollow and they didn't know it. When one of the boys got on the zipline, the tree finally cracked and fell on top of my niece and killed her.

I was just in shock. I told my mom, "I'll get a flight first thing in the morning, and I'll be there as soon as I can." I turned to my husband and told him what had happened and that I needed to get to New Jersey. I didn't sleep at all that night, and I got to the airport as early as possible the next morning to get on a flight. When I got to the gate, I talked to the attendant and asked, "I noticed that the seat I got assigned is a middle seat. Is there any way I could possibly get a seat by myself where I don't have to talk to anyone? I've been up all night and am headed to a family emergency." She said, "Sorry, Ma'am. But this is a completely full flight. I don't know that there is anything I can possibly do. But why don't you go have a seat and I'll let you know if anything comes up."

I went and took a seat for a bit, and a little later she called me up and said, "Ma'am, here's your new seat assignment. I wasn't able to get you by yourself, but this seat is right behind first class with a little extra room, and you will be by the window."

So, I took my bag and headed on board. I went in, and there was a younger white man in the aisle seat and an older African-American woman in the middle. I took my seat by the window.

All I wanted to do was fluff up my pillow and lay my head down and rest. I was so exhausted from a lack of sleep at this point. As I went to lay my head down, this woman in the middle was just looking at me and smiling. I thought, "Oh Lord, no. I can't talk with anyone right now. I just need some peace and quiet, Lord." I just laid my head down, and occasionally I would open my eyes and look over, and this woman was still just looking at me and smiling. At this point I had to at least acknowledge her.

I said, "Hi, I'm really sorry, but I just can't talk to anyone right now." She said, "It's okay, honey, but we need to get you well before you go see your sister." I said, "Okay." Without even thinking I grabbed my Bible, and she started going through Scripture with me and talking to me about the peace that surpasses all understanding. I couldn't believe what had just happened. In a matter of seconds I went from being halfway asleep to being ministered to by this woman on the plane.

Through this woman I felt the presence of the Holy Spirit, and a great sense of peace came over me. She was amazing! It was the most unexpected plane ride that brought me such an incredible sense of peace in one of the most tragic times. The craziest part was that she mentioned the need "to get me well before I see my sister" before I had told her anything about my situation.

When we finally landed in New Jersey and unloaded from the plane, we said our goodbyes. I just remember giving her the biggest hug and thanking her for taking the time to comfort me and walk through Scripture with me. As I walked down to the baggage claim, I was blown away by how God had provided for my needs during this flight. And as I thought about it, I remembered that I wasn't even supposed to be sitting next to this woman. The attendant was the one who had randomly moved me to this particular seat next to this special angel, and God had provided the divine appointment.

When my friend picked me up, the first thing I did was tell her all about this angel I had met on the plane. Then, when I finally got to my mom's house and dropped my bags in the bedroom, the first thing I did was call my girlfriends back in Florida who had been praying for me to tell them about this angel on the plane. When I told my friend Judy, she just started sobbing. She said, "Michele, we all got together and prayed for someone to be with you on the plane who could comfort you and give you strength. That's exactly what we prayed for."

I ended up being in New Jersey with my sister for two weeks, and I didn't break down once. While my sister was going through all the emotions herself, I was able to be her strength. I was able to help her and my brother-in-law make difficult decisions and handle all the details during that time. Jesus used me during that time to lift her up. At one point my sister was sitting in their family room bawling, and she refused to go into the kitchen because when they brought her daughter into the house they took her to the kitchen and she was lying there covered in blood until the paramedics showed up. Something just came over me, and without even thinking I said, "Maria, that blood that was all over Rachel was the blood of Christ. Jesus covered your daughter in that moment and brought her up with Him to heaven." I honestly couldn't believe what had just come out of my mouth. It was from the Holy Spirit.

My sister ended up spending a great deal of time in her Bible and praying with her Bible study girlfriends. Even at her own daughter's funeral she told everyone, "If you don't know Jesus. You need to know Him now. It's only because of Him that my daughter is in heaven right now. Jesus is alive, and my baby girl is with Him." She shared a testimony of God's love with everyone at her daughter's funeral.

It was around the time of the funeral that I told my sister about the woman on the plane. After I described this woman to her, she immediately told me a story about a woman she had met at the hospital. She said, "While I was waiting in this room, a nurse came in very abruptly, rudely, and very matter-of-factly and said, 'You need to come with me and say good bye to your daughter.' She had such a harsh way about her, I just said, 'I don't know who you are, but I'm not going anywhere with you, and I'm not saying good bye to my daughter with you.'"

Then my sister said that a little later another woman walked in, and she described her as an older African-American woman who looked just like the woman I had described to her from the plane. My sister said, "She came in the room slowly and gently and said, 'Maria, would you please come with me? Let's go pray over your daughter. We'll pray together.' We went down to the room together where my daughter was lying, and we prayed together over her body and I said my good-byes." It blows me away to think about the divine appointments God lined up all along this journey.

> Look for a need and meet it.
> Find a hurt and heal it.
> Be alert to the cry for help and answer it.
> Listen for the voice of God and speak it.
> Identify someone's weakness and overcome it.
> Look for what's missing and supply it.
> When you do, the power of God
> —the energizing, enabling,
> charismatic activity of the Holy Spirit—
> will equip you . . . (Sam Storms)

Final reminders:

- God used shepherds; fishermen; tax collectors; and, most importantly, a carpenter. The only requirement is to have a heart for God.
- God wants to set you afire with passion that burns for loving people and engaging people with the heart of Christ.
- Christianity is not a constant state of proving our love for God; it's a constant state of being in love with God.
- We need to wake up to the full reality of Christ in our lives and let the Holy Spirit out of His compartmentalized cage!
- When we partner with the Holy Spirit, we go from ordinary men and women to agents of God's mighty power.
- An exciting firsthand adventure with God is vital to the life of faith for every believer.
- Ultimately, a boring testimony leads to a boring faith.
- Firsthand experiences with God take us from partial faith to fullness of faith, from wimpy Christianity to powerful Christianity.
- May God give you the power to accomplish all the good things your faith prompts you to do.
- Be doers of God's Word, not just hearers.
- It's not God who is cruelly withholding Himself from people's lives. It's us Christians who are the cruel ones withholding ourselves and Christ-in-us from people's lives.
- All we can do is seek to bless and release. Bless others with love, care, and prayer. Then release them and the results into the hands of our heavenly Father.
- Let your positive comments run wild and give the Holy Spirit an opportunity to parlay those positive sentiments into divine appointments.

DISCUSSION QUESTIONS

1. In the section "The Power of the Prompt to See the Need," which question prompt would you be the most likely to try out? Here's your challenge: find someone to try that prompt with in the next 24 hours.

2. In the section "The Power of Care to Plant the Seed," which of the five love languages are you most competent and comfortable with? Here's your challenge: find someone to engage with that love language (words of affirmation, quality time, acts of service, or gift giving), as you've done in the past, but this time try to go the extra mile. Look for a way to take this act of kindness to the next level with some additional creativity, thoughtfulness, or additional effort.

3. In the section "The Power of Prayer to Call God to the Deed," it is noted that prayer gives you the opportunity to properly cite the source of your love, care, and concern. What are your thoughts about Christians doing good things *without* using the name of the Lord—whether intentionally or otherwise? Christians often do good and get all the credit. How can we find a balance, so that we can give God as much glory as possible and allow others to recognize the experience as a God encounter instead of merely a good encounter? Here's the challenge: the next time you find yourself engaging in a good encounter, be intentional about turning the interaction toward God—whether through thanksgiving, prayer, spiritual check-in, etc.

A Prayer for Tapping into the Unlimited Potential of Christ

2 Thessalonians 1:11–12

With this in mind, we constantly pray for you, that our God may make you worthy of his calling, and that by his power he may bring to fruition your every desire for goodness and your every deed prompted by faith. We pray this so that the name of our Lord Jesus may be glorified in you, and you in him, according to the grace of our God and the Lord Jesus Christ.

Ephesians 1:16–20

I have not stopped giving thanks for you, remembering you in my prayers. I keep asking that the God of our Lord Jesus Christ, the glorious Father, may give you the Spirit of wisdom and revelation, so that you may know him better. I pray that the eyes of your heart may be enlightened in order that you may know the hope to which he has called you, the riches of his glorious inheritance in his holy people, and his incomparably great power for us who believe. That power is the same as the mighty strength he exerted when he raised Christ from the dead and seated him at his right hand in the heavenly realms.

Ephesians 3:14–21

For this reason I kneel before the Father, from whom every family in heaven and on earth derives its name. I pray that out of his glorious riches he may strengthen you with power through his Spirit in your inner being, so that Christ may dwell in your hearts through faith. And I pray that you, being rooted and established in love, may have power, together with all the Lord's holy people, to grasp how wide and long and high and deep is the love of Christ, and to know this love that surpasses knowledge—that you may be filled to the measure of all the fullness of God.

Now to him who is able to do immeasurably more than all we ask or imagine, according to his power that is at work within us, to him be glory in the church and in Christ Jesus throughout all generations, for ever and ever! Amen.

About the Author

Dr. Ryan Montague, PhD, is an associate professor in the Department of Communication at Azusa Pacific University. Ryan focuses his research, writing, and speaking on the initiation, development, and sustainability of personal relationships. His areas of emphasis include divine opportunities, emotional and social intelligence, dating and spouse selection, marital communication, and genuine dialogue. Ryan and his family live in greater Los Angeles, California.

Acknowledgements

David Watson, thank you for your spiritual mentorship and guidance. God has used you to introduce divine appointments into the lives of so many people. We are all blessed by your heart for people and obedience to God. You've paved the way and allowed me to have a healthy, motivated, and miraculous introduction to this topic that has made everything else possible.

Tim Beals (Credo House Publishers), thank you for your trust, openness, and expertise which has made publishing this book possible. You always add a much-needed level of professionalism to each book. God has called and equipped you to the art of publishing and I am so grateful that He connected our paths. You are an answer to prayer, as God has used you to open a door for me into this publishing world.

Philip and Holly Wagner (Oasis Church LA), you have pastored and raised up some of the most incredible people in my life. God used you to disciple a generation of pastors around Los Angeles. I have been the recipient of blessings, teachings, and friendships that directly link back to you. You have no idea how fully and widely God has used you. And you won't know until you get to heaven and God reveals all the ripple effects of your faith. So, thank you for your faithfulness, investment, and leadership in so many people's lives.

Thank you to all of my students at Azusa Pacific University over the past eight years. You all have endured so many teachings, conversations, and stories of divine appointments and missed opportunities. Your thoughts, reflections, questions, comments, and stories have informed my writing in countless ways. I have treasured my time with you all and I am so grateful to have been your professor.

Thank you to Azusa Pacific University for funding a sabbatical so that I could have the time and attention to devote to this work. It was during the sabbatical that I experienced more divine appointments in three months than I had experienced in the previous three years. Thank you for encouraging all the research and teaching in these areas of life, faith, and ministry.

Thank you to my family at Redeemed Life Church. You all are amazing, hilarious, loving, and incredibly supportive of our family. You all have showed us that "there is nothing like the church, when the church is being the church," as Pastor Anthony puts it.